To Gail, Kelly, Brian, and Michelle
Harry, Sara, Michael, and Sarah

CONTENTS

Preface   vii

PART ONE   *PRINCIPLES*   1

Chapter 1
The Process of Human Communication   3

The Importance of Human Communication   6
What Is Human Communication?   7
Box 1.1 Techno-Etiquette   8
A Model of Human Communication   9
Communication Contexts   17
Communication Technologies   20
What Is Effective Communication?   21

Chapter 2
Person Perception   33

Perceiving People and Objects: A Comparison   35
Forming Impressions   40
Box 2.1 Self-Concept East and West: Who Are You?   44
Some Variables Involved in Accurate Perception   59
Improving Perception and Communication   61

Chapter 3
The Verbal Message   67

Words and Meaning   68
Message Encoding: A Child's Use of Language   75
Box 3.1 A Word about Semantics   76
Language and Thought   81
Words in Action   90

Chapter 4
The Nonverbal Message   103

Interpreting Nonverbal Messages   104
Spatial and Temporal Cues   108
Visual Cues   116
Box 4.1 Faking It?   120
Vocal Cues   129
Deception   133

Chapter 5
Listening   141

Why Listen?   142
Importance of Listening   144
Box 5.1 Listening: The Forgotten Skill   145
What Is Meant by Listening   146
Types of Listening   150
How to Improve Listening   156

Chapter 6
Conflict and Negotiation   165

Conflict   166
Box 6.1 Conflict and Negotiation   167
Negotiation   177

Chapter 7
Ethics and Communication   193

Principles   194
Issues   198
Box 7.1 Can We Censor Hate?   206
Box 7.2 Revealing Group Secrets   208

Chapter 8
Relationships in Process   219

Bases of Human Attraction   220
Defining Characteristics of Relationships   225
Box 8.1 Platonic Friendships   233
Theories of Relationship Development   236

Maintaining Relationships   242
Family Communication   246

PART TWO   *CONTEXTS*   255

Chapter 9
Interpersonal Communication   257

The Social Setting   258
The Dialectics of Relationships   262
Assessing the Quality of an Interpersonal
   Relationship   265
Box 9.1 Love's Prototypes and Scripts   272

Chapter 10
Intercultural Communication   293

A Definition of Culture   294
Some Dimensions of Cultural Difference   297
Obstacles to Intercultural Communication   303
Barriers to Intercultural Understanding   314
Box 10.1 Some Guidelines for Critical Viewers
   of Film and Television   318
Effects of Intercultural Communication   322

Chapter 11
Interviewing   331

Standardized and Unstandardized Interviews
   335
Types of Interview Questions   335
Box 11.1 Interviewing: Conversation with a
   Purpose   336
Suspect Questions and How to Handle Them
   340
Types of Inadequate Responses   341
Interview Structure   343
Nondirective Interview Technique   346
Helpful Hints   348

Chapter 12
Small-Group Communication   355

Types of Small Groups   357
Group Dynamics   358

Group Structure   372
Correlates of Effective Groups   379
Box 12.1 The Value of Work Teams   383

Chapter 13
Public Communication   391

A Definition   392
The Speaker   395
The Audience   406
The Message   411
Box 13.1 Sample Speech   434
Box 13.2 Sample Speech   436

Chapter 14
Organizational Communication   447

Organizations: A Definition   448
Organizational Culture   450
Importance of Communication   452
Box 14.1 Power in Organizations   462

Chapter 15
Mass Communication and the New
Technologies   479

A First Definition   480
The Process of Mass Communication   485
Box 15.1 Media Conglomerates   488
Box 15.2 The Journalism of Attachment   492
Some Effects and Outcomes   498
Box 15.3 Advertising and Public Relations
   504
Implications of the New Communication
   Technologies   510

Glossary   G–1
References   R–1
Credits   C–1
Indexes
   Name Index   I–1
   Subject Index   I–6

PREFACE

This ninth edition of *Human Communication* is designed to give students a broad-based and up-to-date survey of the entire discipline. Our commitment is to present students with a comprehensive theoretical base, an understanding of how modern communication has evolved and continues to change and grow, and a grasp of its immediate and long-term applications to their own lives.

We focus on the traditional concerns of speech communication and link together contexts as various as interpersonal, intercultural, and mass communication. Our approach is to fuse current and classical communication theory, fundamental concepts, and important skills. We believe that we can present the increasingly complex subject of communication to introductory students without oversimplification and in language that is clear, vivid, and precise.

We have tried to create a text that is sensitive to diversity and that reflects our long-term interest in gender and cultural issues. Throughout our book we draw on and integrate examples and references representing people from a wide variety of backgrounds, ages, and ethnic and cultural groups.

NEW TO THIS EDITION

- NEW ORGANIZATION. One of the major changes in this ninth edition is the new order of some chapters. In response to student and reviewer suggestions, to achieve greater continuity we have placed the Relationships chapter just before the Interpersonal Communication chapter.
- ENHANCED VISUALS. The text features an enhanced visual program including illustrations of high- and low-contact

cultures, postural cues, Knapp's staircase model, Duck's stages, U.S. immigration: 1890–2000, and high- and low-context cultures.
- SEPTEMBER 11, 2001. The events of September 11, 2001, are examined in the Mass Communication and Intercultural chapters.
- TECHNOLOGY. Expanded coverage of technology in this edition includes more critical descriptions of useful websites throughout, and the book's new Online Learning Center at *www.mhhe.com/tubbsmoss*. The Online Learning Center provides a variety of resources and activities for students and instructors. Icons at the end of each chapter prompt the reader to go online for a rich variety of resources and activities, including interactive review quizzes and glossary flashcards.
- KEY TERMS. In addition to the glossary at the end of the book, we have added a key terms list at the end of each chapter to make it easier for students to study the material.

These revisions are very much a response to current theories, issues, and research in communication. This edition has been thoroughly updated and includes many new citations, a new design, and new photographs.

Plan of the Book

Chapter 1 introduces the process of human communication. New, fresh content includes findings based on 25 years of research that identify discernible differences between average job performers and top job performers; information about how electronic technologies have influenced the communication arena; new information on how the use of e-mail in daily lives can create e-stress; new research on the average use of cell phones among teenagers; and finally, a self-test that can indicate whether or not one has become addicted to the Internet.

Chapter 2, on person perception, examines how we learn to view ourselves, how we form impressions of others, and how accurate our perceptions can be. Revisions include greater coverage of self-concept and self-esteem, new research on shyness in college students, and a study of the relationship between shyness and Internet use. There also is new material on how people form impressions of others online and how stereotyping relates to body image and to intercultural communication.

Chapter 3, on the elements of verbal communication, cites the new language movement called Words Can Heal as an example of the growing awareness of the positive and negative power of words. Chapter 3 presents the origin of the term "spam" and how it came into conflict with Hormel Foods Corporation. In addition, there is new discussion of the impact of communication on self-concept and overall life effectiveness, and developing relabeling skills to improve self-talk.

In **Chapter 4,** we have streamlined and updated our treatment of nonverbal communication by adding new areas of interest and current research as well as new examples, some drawn from contemporary drama and fiction. In looking at spatial cues, we also discuss high- and low-contact cultures. There is also fresh material on tempo, eye movements, body movements, and conceptions of time. The revised section on touch now includes touch avoidance. And the new information on vocal cues—including the "what sounds beautiful is good" hypothesis—discusses how they affect our responses to voice mail and answering machines. The chapter also has new illustrations designed to optimize reader interest.

Chapter 5, on listening, discusses the types of listening and provides practical tips for improving listening competencies.

Chapter 6, dealing with conflict and negotiation, has new material recognizing the importance of negotiation and conflict management in the aftermath of the September 11, 2001, World Trade Center and Pentagon attacks.

In **Chapter 7,** we look at ethics as a continuum that extends from interpersonal to mass communication, and we expand the compass of our discussion to include several challenging issues raised by new technologies. We examine excuses given for lying and the effects of "white lies." Misrepresentation is considered not only as it relates to the mass media but to personal and online relationships. There also is fresh material on censorship, hate sites, and online bigotry. Our coverage of secrets, disclosures, and privacy now includes how the mass media report on politicians and the surveillance of computer users.

Chapter 8, (formerly Chapter 6) on relationship processes presents new research on changing preferences in mate selection, as well as revised sections on confirmation and supportiveness. Knapp's theory about relationship stages and Duck's theory about how relationships deteriorate have been rewritten to be more accessible, and Knapp's staircase model is now supported by a new illustration. Also revised and expanded are the sections on maintaining relationships, on friendship, and on romantic relationships. In the final section on family communication, we now discuss some of the unique problems of stepfamilies. This chapter has been revised to dovetail more effectively with Chapter 9 on interpersonal communication. As a result, the section on relationship dialectics now appears in that chapter.

Chapter 9 on interpersonal communication—the first of our chapters on communication contexts—has been substantially revised and has many new examples throughout, some of which are drawn from contemporary literature.

In addition to the new section on the dialectical approach, there is new material on self-disclosure. The revised discussion of intimacy includes coverage of attachment styles and synthesizes research on intimacy between siblings. New material on commitment and on theories about love includes Sternberg's love triangles and the work of Lee and Hendrick and Hendrick on love styles. A self-test for students brings these studies to life. The concluding section on dominance, status, and power has a new discussion of power and equity in marriage—and also examines assertive communication as distinct from nonassertive and aggressive communication.

In **Chapter 10** on intercultural communication, we have added a new section on the three major approaches to this vital area of study. There is also new material on conflict norms, as well as revised and expanded sections on ethnocentrism and stereotyping. This chapter also addresses the issues of bigotry (e.g., anti-Arab sentiment) and group polarization and the Internet. We discuss tolerance and a new research project on community building. Other changes include a map on high- and low-context cultures, a table on links between hate sites on the Web, and guidelines for critical viewing of film and television.

Chapter 11, on interviewing, provides information on how to prepare for job interviews and includes a new discussion of the worst mistakes that interviewees make during job interviews. New material on strategic interviewing and the STAR method gives the reader tips for optimizing success in interviews. We have included a checklist to use in preparing for an interview.

Chapter 12, on small-group communication, offers a new leadership assessment, coverage of new trends such as "Meeting-Free Fridays," and a new research-based summary of the eight correlates of high-performing teams. There also is fresh coverage of emotional intelligence and the characteristics of effective group leaders.

Chapter 13, on public communication, offers new tips from David Gergen, former speechwriter for presidents Richard Nixon, Gerald Ford, Ronald Reagan, and Bill Clinton. To illustrate source credibility, it includes new excerpts from one of General Colin Powell's speeches. In addition there is new material covering persuasion, use-of-fear appeals, tips for improving delivery, research findings on the use of PowerPoint, and a new sample speech from President Bush to Congress following the September 11, 2001, terrorist attacks.

Chapter 14, on organizational communication, includes new material based on Gallup surveys of over one million people across 400 countries and on the work of Daniel Goleman at Harvard who asserts that communication skills account for 85 to 90 percent of a leader's success. A new section on change management skills gives direction to people who are not in top leadership positions. Within a discussion on change, a case concerning Continental Airlines is used to describe how its new CEO chose a radical method to communicate a shift in the corporation's culture.

Our many changes in **Chapter 15** on mass media and the new technologies include increased coverage of media conglomerates, revised coverage of ethics and censorship, new material on media uses and gratifications, as well as research on the diffusion of information following the events of September 11, 2001. There is also new information on attitude influence and politics and an updated section on media representations of women in the worlds of work and technology. The section concerning media violence now discusses the mean world syndrome and the third-person effect. We also examine new research on the effects of technology on interpersonal communication, recent findings on the digital divide, and the use of the new technologies to implement political and social change.

RESOURCES

Human Communication incorporates several teaching aids that we hope will be of benefit to both students and their instructors: Each chapter begins with *Student Objectives*, and concludes with a *Summary*, a list of *Key Terms*, a set of *Review Questions*, and a set of *Exercises*. Each chapter also includes an *Issues in Communication* box to serve as a source for classroom discussion and possible student assignments. Half of the Issues boxes are new to this edition. These chapter pedagogies are supported by the text's new *FREE Online Learning Center, www.mhhe.com/tubbsmoss*, which provides activities and teaching and study resources for both instructors and students.

Annotations for the end-of-chapter *Suggested Readings* feature, which includes popular and scholarly readings, have been thoroughly updated. The *Instructor's Manual* and the *Test File* have also been revised and updated for the ninth edition.

Please contact your local McGraw-Hill representative to learn about other resources and options for this text, such as custom publishing, online editions, and acquiring or developing content for course management systems such as BlackBoard and WebCT. To locate your local representative, visit *www.mhhe.com* and select Rep Locator.

For their valuable reviews and critiques of the ninth edition we wish to thank:

Gary Meyer, *Marquette University*
Heidi M. Rose, *Villanova University*
Karen Buzzard, *Northeastern University*
Rebecca Parker, *Western Illinois University*
Larry J. Whatule, *University of Pittsburgh at Greensburg*
Karen C. Evans, *Ohio University, Lancaster Campus*
Carey Noland, *Ohio State University*

We wish to express our gratitude to our editors at McGraw-Hill: Nanette Kauffman and Jennie Katsaros for their commitment, support, and invaluable contributions to this project; to Rebecca Nordbrock for skillfully guiding our manuscript through the intricacies of editing and production; and to Jenny El-Shamy for the exquisite new cover and interior design for this edition.

Stewart Tubbs
Sylvia Moss

Stewart L. Tubbs

Stewart L. Tubbs is the Darrell H. Cooper Professor of Leadership in the College of Business at Eastern Michigan University and former Dean of the College of Business. He received his doctorate in Communication and Organizational Behavior from the University of Kansas. His master's degree in Communication and his bachelor's degree in Science are from Bowling Green State University. He has completed postdoctoral work in management at the University of Michigan, Harvard Business School, and Stanford Graduate School of Business.

Dr. Tubbs has also taught at General Motors Institute, and at Boise State University, where he was Chairman of the Management Department and, later, Associate Dean of the College of Business.

He has been named an Outstanding Teacher four times, has consulted extensively for *Fortune* 500 companies, and is former Chairman of the Organizational Communication division of the Academy of Management. In 1994, he received the Outstanding Leadership Award in London from the Academy of Business Administration and was also inducted into the Distinguished Alumni Hall of Fame by Lakewood High School in Lakewood, Ohio.

Dr. Tubbs is the author of *A Systems Approach to Small Group Interaction* and co-author of *Interpersonal Communication* with Sylvia Moss. He is listed in *American Men and Women of Science, Contemporary Authors, Directory of American Scholars,* the *International Who's Who in Education,* and *Outstanding Young Men of America.*

Sylvia Moss

Sylvia Moss is a professional writer with a strong interest in the social sciences. She received her undergraduate education at Barnard College and the University of Wisconsin and holds graduate degrees from Columbia University and New York University. She is the author, with Stewart Tubbs, of *Interpersonal Communication* and has contributed to several college textbooks in the social sciences.

A writing consultant, Ms. Moss has taught at the College of New Rochelle and has also taught writing workshops. A collection of her poetry, *Cities in Motion,* was selected by Derek Walcott for The National Poetry Series and published by the University of Illinois Press. Selections from her work also appear in *Six Poets* (St. Petersburg) as well as in the *Grolier Poetry Prize Annual* and such literary journals as *New Letters, Helicon Nine,* and *Foreign Literature* (Moscow). She is the recipient of a Whiting Writer's Award and has twice been a Yaddo Fellow. She is the editor of *China 5000 Years: Innovation and Transformation in the Arts,* published by the Guggenheim Museum.

PART ONE
Principles

The Process of Human Communication

1

Chapter Objectives

After reading this chapter, you should be able to:

1. Define the term "communication."
2. Describe what is referred to by the term "input" as it is used in the communication model.
3. List four types of messages and give an example of each type.
4. Distinguish between technical and semantic interference and give an example of each.
5. Describe the impact of feedback on behavior.
6. Identify seven different contexts of communication and explain how each is distinctive.
7. Define effective communication in terms of five possible outcomes of human communication.

The tragic events of September 11, 2001, in New York, Washington, D.C., and Pennsylvania have changed us all. One of the lessons from those events has been the important role of communication in informing and uniting the citizens of this country and other countries. Never before has the discipline of human communication been a more important or relevant field of study. We sincerely hope that this book will help you in achieving all of your communication objectives.

On a less tragic but also significant topic, a 23-year-old woman named Julia Butterfly Hill decided to send a message. She felt passionate about the environment and decided that in order to save one giant redwood tree from being cut down she would live 180 feet up in the tree. She stayed in the tree for 738 days! Think about it. She spent over two years of her life to send a message. However, through her dedication and passive methods, she was able to reach an agreement with the logging companies to develop better methods for preserving the rights and interest of both parties. Later she was featured in *People* magazine's "25 Most Intriguing People of the Year." You can read more in her book (Hill, 2000) or click on *www.circleoflifefoundation.org.*

Another story is told that a woman was given the opportunity to meet two of the most famous men in England, William Gladstone and Benjamin Disraeli. Afterward she was asked her impressions. She said that after meeting Gladstone she was convinced that she had been talking to the most important person in England. However, after meeting Disraeli, she said that she was convinced that she was the most important person in England.

Perhaps this is the most important example that we can offer about how to be a successful communicator. Throughout this book, we will be offering many examples and concepts as well as practical guidelines designed to help you improve your communication. We sincerely hope that you can accomplish this objective.

For many years it has been thought that the speech function was unique to modern Homo sapiens. However, just within the past few years, evidence has been found that indicates that the first creatures to use spoken communication were Neanderthals, or more ancient Homo sapiens dating back 60,000 years. Garrett (1989) reports: "Now an international research team has found what it believes is the Neanderthal version of a bone that is a key to modern human speech . . . Baruch Arensburg of Tel Aviv University and his team unearthed the hyoid bone while digging in Israel's Kebara cave . . . The hyoid is a U-shaped bone that supports the tongue and its muscles" (p. 560).

Begley and Gleizes (1989) report this additional evidence:

Early Orators: Although Neanderthal's brain was bigger than ours, ever since his discovery "he was considered dull-witted and inarticulate," says neuroanatomist Terrence Deacon of Harvard University. Now that prejudice is yielding. Fossil brain casts show a well-developed language area, says Dean Falk of the State University of New York at Albany. His speech was only slightly inferior: using skull fossils to infer the position of the voice box in early humans, . . . Neanderthals had a more restricted vocal range than we do. They had nasal voices, but could probably pronounce every consonant and vowel sound except "oo" and "ee," adds Deacon. "They were articulate, intelligent humans we would be able to understand and interact with," he says. (p. 71)

Fast forward. Today, most people complain that they are overloaded with too much communication. According to one study by Pitney-Bowes Inc. and the Institute for the Future (Clark, 1999), the average U.S. office worker sends and receives 201 messages a day through various means. This breaks down as follows:

52 telephone calls

32 e-mails

22 voice mail messages

18 interoffice mail pieces

18 U.S. Postal Service mail pieces

15 faxes

11 post-it notes

10 telephone message slips

4 overnight letters/packages

4 messages by pagers

3 U.S. Postal Service Express Mail deliveries

3 cellular phone calls

One participant in this study responded, "If we don't respond, we become the weak link in the communications chain" (p. R4).

More recently, consulting firms have sprung up to help deal with "e-stress." Walkabout Excursions of Ann Arbor, Michigan, is one such firm. A study released by the Gartner Group says that 42 percent of corporate users check their business e-mail while on vacation, while 23 percent check e-mail on weekends. On workdays, 53 percent of business users check e-mail six or more times a day. Maurice Caplan Grey, Gartner senior research analyst said that, "The thought of communication happening without our knowledge keeps us tethered to the workplace" (Wendland, 2001). If you would like to join an online discussion about coping with information overload, see *www.wsi.com.*

Keep in mind that all these messages do not even include all the interpersonal communication events we experience. It is no wonder that we need to learn more about human communication!

For over 60,000 years men and women have been communicating. Yet we still feel the need, perhaps more than ever, to find ways to improve these skills. This book is dedicated to that end.

THE IMPORTANCE OF HUMAN COMMUNICATION

According to numerous research studies, for your entire life you have spent about 75 percent of each day engaged in communication. Therefore, you may be wondering why you need to study communication in the first place. There is a good reason: Quantity is no guarantee of quality. Given the number of divorces, unhappy workers, and ruptured parent-to-offspring relationships, quantity and frequency of communication are clearly no measure of how effectively people communicate with each other.

Despite the difficulties inherent in ordinary communication, some researchers are attempting communication with an unborn child. Laitner (1987) reports that in Hayward, California, the Prenatal University (PU) was founded by obstetrician–gynecologist Dr. Rene Van de Carr. His work involves teaching babies in the uterus, thus giving them a head start on verbal ability and social skills. Parents talk to their children through paper megaphones directed at the mother's abdomen. Research conducted on PU graduates showed that they "were communicating significantly earlier, and they used compound words earlier, and the mother felt they understood things earlier." However, a warning about pushing children too fast has been issued by the American Academy of Pediatrics. Dr. Robert Sokol, chairman of the Department of Obstetrics and Gynecology at Wayne State University in Detroit, says that "there is no evidence that (fetuses) can process language" (p. 2B).

At the other end of the life spectrum, Morse and Perry (1990) report on the near-death experiences of several dozen people who have survived death and come back to tell about their communication experiences. Reading their book is like watching the movie *Ghost:* It extends the boundaries of our knowledge of communication even beyond death.

Among other things, communication has been linked to **physical well-being.** Stewart (1986) indicates that socially isolated people are more likely to die prematurely; divorced men die at double the normal rate from cancer, heart disease, and strokes, five times the normal rate from hypertension, five times the normal rate from suicide, seven times the normal rate from cirrhosis of the liver, and ten times the normal rate from tuberculosis. Also, poor communication skills have been found to contribute to coronary heart disease, and the likelihood of death increases when a marriage partner dies.

Communication is also closely associated with one's **definition of self.** Rosenberg (1979) relates the story of the "wild boy of Aveyron" who was raised by wolves. He developed no identity as a human being until he began to interact with humans. Individuals gain a sense of self-identity by being paid attention to and getting feedback from others. Also, a sense of identity and worth develops from comparing ourselves with others.

General education needs revolve around communication. The highly regarded Carnegie Foundation for the Advancement of Teaching has recommended that teaching communication be one of the highest possible priorities for undergraduate education. Communication was the only subject field identified in their recommendations! (Kenny, 1998)

On-the-job communication is constantly cited as one of the most important skills in "getting ahead." Whetten and Cameron (2002) identified 402 individuals who were rated as highly effective managers in their own organizations in such fields as business, health care, education, and government. They then interviewed the individuals to determine what attributes were associated with their effectiveness. The table below shows the top ten list of most frequently cited skills of effective managers.

Most Frequently Cited Skills of Effective Managers

1. Oral Communication (including listening)
2. Managing time and stress
3. Managing individual decisions
4. Recognizing, defining, and solving problems
5. Motivating and influencing others
6. Delegating
7. Setting goals and articulating a vision
8. Self-awareness
9. Team building
10. Managing conflict (p. 8)

As you will see, many of these topics are covered in this book.

These research findings have been confirmed by a 10-year study conducted by researchers at Carnegie Mellon University, which identified the most important skills that differentiated between average job performers and outstanding job performers (Kelley, 1998). They found that interpersonal communication, relationship building, leadership, teamwork, networking, and persuasion were some of the most important skills for job performance career success.

In this book, we shall be exploring each of these aspects of human communication—all the way from the first impressions we form of one another to how human relationships are maintained and sometimes terminated.

WHAT IS HUMAN COMMUNICATION?

What do you think of when the word "communication" is used? Students answering this question may mention anything from the use of electric circuits to prayer. Communication is a subject so frequently discussed that the term itself has become too meaningful—that is, it has too many different meanings for people. Agreeing on a working definition is the first step toward improving our understanding of this complex phenomenon.

1.1 ISSUES IN COMMUNICATION

Techno-Etiquette

What are some of the complications that have arisen as a result of the increased communication through such media as telephones, cellular phones, fax messages, and e-mail? How do you resolve some of the difficulties? Audrey Glassman (1998) has raised some of the following issues:

Telephones

1. How do you feel when you are on a call and someone takes another call on "call waiting"?
2. How do you feel when someone puts you on a speaker phone and your side of the conversation is more or less public?

Cellular Phones

3. Have you ever had any unusual experiences in which a person is talking on a car phone while driving?
4. Can you think of any situations in which it is appropriate to receive cellular phone calls when you are in a movie theater?

Fax Messages

5. When is it appropriate to send your résumé by fax if you are applying for a job?
6. Should you send confidential messages by fax? Are there any exceptions?

E-mail Messages

7. How many pages long should your messages usually be?
8. Have you ever had your message forwarded to someone you didn't expect? What should you do to anticipate this?
9. Have you ever sent a message when you were angry? Have you learned anything from this?

Communication has been broadly defined as "the sharing of experience," and to some extent all living organisms can be said to share experience. What makes human communication unique is the superior ability to create and to use symbols, for it is this ability that enables humans to share experiences indirectly and vicariously. A symbol can be defined as something used for or regarded as representing something else. For the time being, though, let us say that human communication is the process of creating a meaning between two or more people. This is at least a partial definition, one we shall want to expand in discussing communication outcomes.

A MODEL OF HUMAN COMMUNICATION

Since human communication is an intangible, ever-changing process, many people find it helpful to use a tangible model to describe that process. Actually, a motion picture would be a better form for modeling communication. As you read this book, think of the model that follows as one frame of a motion picture—a momentary pause in an ongoing process. The model is not an end in itself; it is only a means to help explain the ways in which the various component parts interact.

Figure 1.1 is a model of the most basic human communication event; it involves only two people. Initially, we shall call them Communicator 1 (the sender/receiver) and Communicator 2 (the receiver/sender). In actuality, both are sources of communication, and each originates and receives messages simultaneously. In addition, both parties are simultaneously being influenced by one another in the transaction. Communicator 1 may originate the first message, and Communicator 2 may be the first person to perceive the transmitted stimuli, but most of our daily communication activities are spontaneous and relatively unstructured, so that these are overlapping roles.

Figure 1.1   *The Tubbs Communication Model*

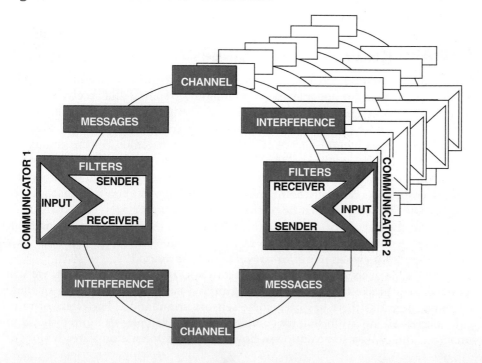

Thus, as represented in the present model, a great many transactions can be initiated from either the right or the left side. For example, when you got up this morning, did you speak to someone first, or were you spoken to first? You probably don't even remember because who spoke first was a matter of chance. In an important sense, it is arbitrary to call yourself either a sender or a receiver: You are both. Even while you are speaking, you are simultaneously observing the other person's behavior and reacting to it. This is also true of the other person as he or she interacts with you.

The transactional view also emphasizes that you change as a result of the communication event. Have you ever been drawn into an argument so intense that the more you told the other person how angry you were, the angrier you became? The reverse is also possible. If a man tells a woman how much he cares for her and goes out of his way to do something thoughtful for her, what is the result? Typically, he increases his feeling of closeness to her, even though she may not respond well to his gesture. The research on self-persuasion shows that when you give a persuasive presentation to others, you are often the person who is most persuaded by it. Alcoholics Anonymous has worked with this principle for many years. The people who get up at meetings and try to persuade others to stay sober are also doing a lot to keep themselves persuaded. The transactional viewpoint, then, emphasizes the simultaneous and mutually influential nature of the communication event. The participants become interdependent, and their communication can be analyzed only in terms of the unique context of the event.

As you read more about our model, keep in mind the transactional viewpoint with its emphasis on the extent to which the two or more people involved create a relationship as part of their communicating.

Communicator 1: Sender/Receiver

Let's take a closer look at Communicator 1, who is trying to transmit a message. Keep in mind that both people are simultaneously sending and receiving all the time. What characteristics of this person would be important in the communication process? Obviously, mental capacities are of central importance. Inside the human brain are millions of nerve cells that function together to store and utilize knowledge, attitudes, and emotions. We want to know what makes Communicator 1 distinct from any other. Like those of any other human being, Communicator 1's senses are continually bombarded by a wealth of stimuli from both inside and outside the body. All that he or she knows and experiences—whether of the physical or the social world—comes initially through the senses. Borrowing from computer terminology, we call these raw data **input**—*all the stimuli, both past and present, that give us our information about the world.*

From the accounts of explorers, castaways, and prisoners of war, we can learn what it is like to experience a long period of isolation, but even in these extreme situations there has been some sensory stimulation. The effect of radically decreased input—in solitary confinement, for example—is more difficult to imagine. You can get some notion of how dependent you are on a steady flow of stimuli by supposing that your senses were shut off one by one. Imagine what it would be like without them for a day or just an hour or even 15 minutes.

Messages

Looking again at the model in Figure 1.1, we can think of the message that Communicator 1 transmits as being conveyed. These messages may be verbal or nonverbal, and they may be intentional or unintentional. Thus four types of messages are possible: (1) intentional verbal, (2) unintentional verbal, (3) intentional nonverbal, and (4) unintentional nonverbal. As we examine these categories individually, keep in mind that most messages contain two or more types of stimuli and that they often overlap.

Verbal Messages   A **verbal message** is *any type of spoken communication that uses one or more words*. Most of the communicative stimuli we are conscious of fall within the category of **intentional verbal messages;** these are *the conscious attempts we make to communicate with others through speech*. Undoubtedly, the most unique aspect of human communication is the use of verbal symbols. It is somewhat of a miracle that we can look at ink marks on a piece of paper or listen to sounds carried on air waves and be able to create images in each other's brains. In fact, the process works so well that we often are surprised when problems occur.

For example, a friend once commented to her mother (who came to this country from Europe) that she had just received a new VISA card. Her mother responded by saying, "Oh really, I didn't know you were planning a trip." To the mother, the term "visa" referred to a permit used to travel to foreign countries. In fact, this "visa" was a charge card. This example serves to illustrate the common principle that words themselves do not contain any meaning. Haney (1992) calls this the "Container Fallacy." In other words, it is a fallacy to believe that meanings are carried or contained by words. If it is possible to have misunderstandings using words that refer to such tangible objects as charge cards, imagine how difficult it is to be able to communicate to another person what we mean by such abstract terms as "truth," "justice," and "fair." Many labor contracts state that if a dispute arises, it must be resolved "within a reasonable period of time." Imagine how much confusion could potentially occur trying to agree on the meaning of "reasonable."

Unintentional verbal messages are *the things we say without meaning to.* Freud argued that all the apparently unintentional stimuli we transmit—both verbal and nonverbal—are unconsciously motivated. We cannot discuss the merits of this argument here, but we can cite an amusing example of a slip of the tongue described by one of Freud's colleagues: "While writing a prescription for a woman who was especially weighed down by the financial burden of the treatment, I was interested to hear her say suddenly: 'Please do not give me *big bills,* because I cannot swallow them.' Of course, she meant to say *pills*" (Freud, 1938, p. 82).

Everyone makes slips occasionally. During an interview with the director of admissions at Lafayette, a candidate was asked why he thought that particular college would be suitable for him. His response was, "Well, I don't want to go to a real big college or a real small college. I just want a mediocre college like Lafayette."

Sometimes it's only when we get feedback from others (laughter, for instance) that we become aware we have transmitted such messages. Even in mass communication, which generally involves a great deal of planning and control, such unintentional messages make their appearance. On a television program, the moderator of a network panel discussion on the safety of nuclear power plants voiced her agreement with one of the panelists. Two days later, letters started arriving from all over the country; viewers were incensed by her lack of objectivity. In general, unintentional stimuli, both verbal and nonverbal, tend to increase in number if the person is a poor communicator. Obviously, those people who represent the mass media are expected to be skilled communicators.

Nonverbal Messages   **Nonverbal messages** cannot be described as easily as verbal messages, probably because the category is so broad. They include all the nonverbal aspects of our behavior: facial expression, posture, tone of voice, hand movements, manner of dress, and so on. In short, *they are all the messages we transmit without words or over and above the words we use*. In the fall of 2001, there was a lot of controversy in high schools regarding the dress code, especially for women. The so-called Britney Spears look with low hip-hugging pants and bare midriff was usually not allowed.

Let us first consider **intentional nonverbal messages,** *the nonverbal messages we want to transmit.* Sometimes we rely exclusively on nonverbal messages to reinforce verbal messages. For example, you can greet someone by smiling and nodding your head, or you can say "Hello" and also smile or wave. At times we deliberately use nonverbal messages to cancel out a polite verbal response and indicate our true feelings: The verbal message may be positive, but the tone and facial expression indicate that we mean something negative.

Much of what we are as a person "communicates" itself every time we behave. Much of this behavior is unintentional. Some writers on the subject go so far as to assert that what we communicate is what we are. **Unintentional nonverbal messages** are *all those nonverbal aspects of our behavior transmitted without our control.* For example, one of the authors once told a student speaker to relax. "I am relaxed," the student replied in a tight voice, trembling, and speaking over the rattling of a paper he was holding. A problem frequently raised in management classes is that store managers unintentionally communicate anger or impatience to their customers.

Controlling nonverbal messages is a very difficult task. Facial expressions, posture, tone of voice, hand gestures—what some writers have called "body language"—often give us away. Ralph Waldo Emerson phrased it well when he remarked to a speaker, "What you are speaks so loudly that I cannot hear what you say." And of course the better a person knows you, the more likely he or she is to pick up your nonverbal expressions—even if you don't want that to happen. Lest we paint too dark a picture, however, we should add that as your communication skills improve, you may find that the number of unintentional messages you transmit will decrease significantly.

Channels

If you are talking on a cell phone, the channel that transmits the communicative stimuli are the air waves via phone towers. The **channels** of face-to-face communication are the sensory organs. Although all five senses may receive the stimuli, you rely almost exclusively on three: hearing, sight, and touch. For example, you listen to someone state an argument, or you exchange knowing glances with a friend, or you put your hand on someone's shoulder. In addition to the sensory organs, the channels of organizational communication include company e-mail messages, newsletters, bulletin boards, printed memoranda, media advertising, and annual reports. In mass communication, the primary channels would be newspapers, films, radio, and television.

In the less formal contexts of communication, we rarely think about communication channels. Usually, a person becomes aware of them only when one or more are cut off or when some sort of interference is present. For example, if there is a large vase of flowers between two people trying to talk across a dinner table, both lose a lot because they are unable to see each other's faces. They may even find it too unsettling to carry on a conversation without the presence of facial cues. In other words, face-to-face communication is a multichannel experience. Simultaneously, we receive and make use of information from a number of different channels. In general, the more channels being used, the greater the number of communicative stimuli transmitted.

Interference

After initiating a message, the sender almost always assumes that it has been received. The sender is puzzled or annoyed if he or she is misinterpreted or gets no response. The sender may even have taken special pains to make the message very clear. "Isn't that enough?" the sender asks. In effect, he or she wants to know what went wrong between the transmission and reception of the message.

The communication scholar would answer, **interference,** or **noise**—that is, *anything that distorts the information transmitted to the receiver or distracts him or her from receiving it.* In communication theory, "interference" and "noise" are synonymous terms. "Interference" is probably a more appropriate word, but because "noise" was the term first used in studies of telecommunication, you should be familiar with it too. One recent example is fashionable clothing. High school dress codes now prohibit clothing that is considered a distraction. This includes plunging necklines, low-riding jeans paired with midriff-baring T-shirts and tops with spaghetti straps (Stone-Palmquist, 2001, p. A1).

Remember that there are many kinds of noise, not just sound. A smoke-filled, overheated classroom, a student who has made abundant use of a very strong perfume, and a lecturer dressed in weird clothing can all become sources of interference.

We can distinguish between two kinds of interference: technical interference and semantic interference. **Technical interference** refers to *the factors that cause the receiver to perceive distortion in the intended information or stimuli*. And the sender too may create the distortion: A person who has a speech impediment or who mumbles a great deal may have difficulty making words clear to someone else. At a party, one person may not be able to hear the response of another because the stereo is blaring or because other people standing nearby are speaking so loudly. In this case, the interference is simply the transmission of the sounds of other people in conversation.

The second type of interference is **semantic interference,** which occurs when *the receiver does not attribute the same meaning to the signal that the sender does*. For example, a city official and a social worker got into a heated argument over the causes of crime. The city official argued that the causes were primarily "economic," and the social worker maintained, quite predictably, that they were largely "social." Only after considerable discussion did the two begin to realize that although they had been using different terms, essentially they were referring to the same phenomenon. Bear in mind, however, that no two people will attribute exactly the same meaning to any word and that it is also possible to attribute different meanings to nonverbal messages.

As we have seen, interference can exist in the context of the communication, in the channel, in the communicator who sends the message, or in the one who receives it. Some interference will always be present in human communication.

Communicator 2: Receiver/Sender

Traditionally, emphasis has been given to the communicator as message sender, but equally important to any viable model of human communication is an analysis of the communicator as receiver. For most communication, visual perception will be an essential aspect of message reception. Another critical aspect of message reception is **listening.**

Listening

There is an ancient Chinese saying, "From listening comes wisdom, from speaking repentance." Listening and hearing are far from synonymous. When Communicator 2 (the receiver/sender) listens, four different yet interrelated processes will be involved: attention, hearing, understanding, and remembering.

Thus far we have discussed the transmission and reception of a single message. At this point, however, our model departs from several current models that create the illusion that all human communication has a definite starting point with a sender and a termination point with a receiver. When the second communicator in Figure 1.1 has received a message, we have come only halfway through the continuous and ongoing process that is communication. For each receiver of a message is also a sender of messages—hence, the term "receiver/sender." Moreover, that person's uniqueness as a human being ensures that his or her attempts to communicate will be very different from those of the other person in the model. For example, Communicator 2's cultural input may be quite unlike that of Communicator 1. His or her filters, both physiological and psychological, will be different. The stimuli he or she transmits will be different. Even the selection of channels and sources of difficulty, or interference, may differ.

The present model includes these differences as inherent parts of the communication process. Although the left half of the model lists the same elements as the right half—input, filters, messages, channels, interference—and these elements are defined in the same way, they are always different in content from those in the right half. The transmission and reception of a single message are only part of our model. Face-to-face communication in particular is characterized by its interdependent participants and the explicit and immediate feedback between them. Even in organizational and mass communication, where the sender/receiver may represent a social organization, the receiver/sender is still able to supply feedback. It may take any number of forms, from a union slowdown in response to the visit of a time-study analyst to an angry letter to the editor of a major newspaper.

Feedback

A common definition of **feedback** is *the return to you of behavior you have generated*. When we examine feedback solely in interpersonal terms, we can be more specific and say that feedback reinforces some behaviors and extinguishes others. For example, one story has it that a psychology instructor who had been teaching the principles of instrumental learning was actually conditioned by his own class. The students decided to give him reinforcement by taking lots of notes, looking attentive, and asking questions whenever he moved to his right. Whenever he moved to his left, they tried to extinguish this behavior by not taking notes, being inattentive, and not asking questions. He was just about teaching from the right front corner of the room when he realized what was happening.

Knapp (1997) has also observed,

many times we talk about our relationships with people as if we had no relation or connection to them—as if our behavior had nothing to do with what the other did. In actuality, however, we have a lot more to do with our partner's responses than we may wish to acknowledge. The reason we often fail to acknowledge this interdependence is that it means we have to accept more of the responsibility for our communication problems. It is much easier to describe your partner's behavior as independent of your own—e.g., "He never listens to me"; "She is never serious with me"; "He doesn't tell me the truth." Acknowledging interdependence forces you to ask yourself what you do to elicit such responses and what you can do to get the responses you desire. Communicators who recognize their interdependence also recognize that communication problems are the result of mutual contribution. One person can't be entirely clean and the other entirely dirty. (p. 11)

Thus, feedback is an essential characteristic of relationships as well as an important source of information about yourself. (If you would like to know more about yourself, check out the Keirsey Temperament Sorter at: *www.keirsey.com/keirsey.html*.)

Time

Once Communicator 2 responds to Communicator 1, their interaction can be represented by a circle. But as their exchange progresses in time, the relationship between them is more accurately described by several circles. In fact, all but the briefest exchanges entail several communication cycles. Thus, time itself becomes the final element in our model.

We have tried to convey the presence of time in Figure 1.1 by representing communication in the form of a spiral, like an uncoiled spring. Some writers prefer to symbolize time as a helix; the only difference between these forms is that the spiral is usually regarded as two-dimensional whereas the helix is thought of as three-dimensional. We shall treat them as identical.

The spiral also illustrates that participants in the communication process can never return to the point at which they started. The relationship must undergo change as a result of each interaction.

Throughout this text, we shall try to point out the effects of time on communication. Implicit in this emphasis is our belief that time is one of the most relevant variables in the study of human communication. If it does nothing else, the spiral or transactional model should remind us that communication is not static and that it thus requires different methods of analysis from a fixed entity.

One author (Tapscott, 1998) has written that an overwhelming majority of those recently surveyed indicate that the pace of life seems to be changing at a more rapid rate than ever before. Thus, the pressures of too much to do in too little time would also appear to be influencing both the quantity and the quality of modern-day communication. If you are interested in looking into this more, log on to *www.technostress.com*.

The model identifies some of the major elements that exist in all human communication. We have discussed such communication only in its simplest form. As we add more communicators, change the kind or amount of interference, or vary the messages transmitted, our subject increases in complexity. We shall see this especially when we turn to the study of communication contexts. As you read on, you may want to look at other models, some of which are mentioned in the books listed at the end of this chapter. You may even want to try your hand at developing a model of your own. In either case remember that each communication event you will study has something unique about it, and no model can be used as a blueprint of the communication process.

COMMUNICATION CONTEXTS

It seems clear that human communication occurs in several kinds of situations. Seven different contexts seem to be widely agreed upon in the communication literature. These are (1) interpersonal, (2) intercultural, (3) interviewing, (4) small group, (5) public communication, (6) organizational communication, and (7) mass communication. Keep in mind that while each of these contexts has some unique characteristics, all of them share in common *the process of creating a meaning between two or more people.* And all of these contexts sometimes involve intercultural communication, another variable we will be examining.

Interpersonal Communication

Interpersonal communication is the basic unit of communication. Although it may occur among three or more individuals in some special circumstances, our communication model depicts this context as occurring between two people. Some scholars believe that the most important defining element in interpersonal communication is the level of closeness or intimacy between the parties. That is felt to be more important than the number of individuals participating. However, we believe that interpersonal communication also includes most of the informal, everyday exchanges that we engage in from the time we get up until the time we go to bed. While a lot of very informal and superficial communication may occur between two people (i.e., a dyad), this is also the context that includes the most intimate relationships we ever experience.

In Mitch Albom's best-selling book *Tuesdays with Morrie,* he tells the true story of his last conversations with his former teacher, Morrie Schwartz, who was dying of ALS (Lou Gehrig's disease). He writes,

> "I don't know why you came back to me. But I want to say this . . ."
> He paused and his voice choked.
> "If I could have had another son, I would have liked it to be you."
> I dropped my eyes, kneading the dying flesh of his feet between my fingers. For a moment I felt afraid, as if accepting his words would somehow betray my own father. But when I looked up, I saw Morrie smiling through tears and I knew there was no betrayal in a moment like this. All I was afraid of was saying goodbye. (Albom, 1997, p. 168)

This passage illustrates the deep love that can develop through interpersonal communication.

Intercultural Communication

In our analysis of human communication, another category we shall be exploring is **intercultural communication**—that is, *communication between members of different cultures (whether defined in terms of racial, ethnic, or socioeconomic* *differences, or a combination of these differences).* **Culture** is *a way of life developed and shared by a group of people and passed down from generation to generation.* Gudykunst and Kim (1992) offer the following example of intercultural communication:

> Consider a visit to North America by strangers from a culture with a communication rule requiring that direct eye contact always be avoided . . . If the strangers do not look them in the eye when talking, the North Americans will assume that the strangers either have something to hide or are not telling the truth. (p. 35)

Similarly, Chin, Gu and Tubbs (2001) write, ". . . being outgoing, as it is normally understood in the U.S., may be perceived as being rude in other cultures, thereby provoking rather than preventing social isolation" (p. 21). Also, Hampden-Turner and Trompenaars (2000) offer a systematic analysis of the communication differences across many cultures.

This dimension of experience cuts across all communication contexts: It may occur in two-person communication, interviews, small groups, or any of the other categories we examine in Part 2. Thus intercultural communication will be discussed not only in Chapter 10 but also in many other chapters of this text—for example, in relation to person perception, human attraction, and verbal and nonverbal communication. In a society such as our own, with its rich mix of cultures, intercultural communication will be especially relevant. (Check out: *www2.soc.hawaii.edu/css/dep...sources/intercultural/splash2.html.*)

Interviewing

An **interview** is often defined as *a communication transaction that emphasizes questions and answers* (Camp and Vielhaber, 2001). Whether it is talking to a physician to help diagnose an illness, to a prospective employer for a job, to a professor for help in a course, to a market researcher to identify strengths in a product, or to a prosecuting attorney on the witness stand, interviewing is often targeted toward accomplishing a specific purpose. Since interviewing is such a stylized form of communication, specific techniques have been developed that can be used to best accomplish the interviewer's purpose. These techniques, along with specific types of interview questions, and so on can be observed on such television programs as *60 Minutes, 20/20,* and *Meet the Press.*

Small-Group Communication

Small-group communication is defined as *"the process by which three or more members of a group exchange verbal and nonverbal messages in an attempt to influence one another"* (Tubbs, 2001, p. 5). Since this context involves three or more people, the degree of intimacy, participation, and satisfaction tends to be lower than in two-person communication. Small-group communication occurs in churches, in social situations, in organizations, and in therapeutic settings, to name a few examples. Group dynamics is a well-researched field of study and tends to focus on small groups that engage in problem solving and decision making. Small-group communication, therefore, tends to focus on the ways to improve the work that can be accomplished in groups. Work teams are but one example of small groups dedicated to improving organizational performance (see Maxwell, 2001).

Public Communication

This context is often referred to as "public speaking." It is a distinct context in a number of ways. First, it occurs in public rather than private places—that is, in auditoriums, classrooms, ballrooms, and so on. Second, public communication is relatively formal as opposed to informal, unstructured communications. Usually, the event is planned in advance. Some people are designated to perform certain functions (such as introducing the speaker). In a commencement exercise, for example, there may be several speakers, as well as a prayer and a ceremony in which degrees are awarded. And third, there are relatively clear-cut behavioral norms (Lucas, 2001). For example, questions are usually addressed to the speaker after the speech is completed. Thus, **public communication** usually requires that the speaker do significantly more preparation, and he or she should expect a more formalized setting than in two-person or small-group communication.

Organizational Communication

Organizational communication is defined as *"the flow of messages within a network of interdependent relationships"* (Goldhaber, 1990, p. 11). This definition fits not only businesses but also hospitals, churches, government agencies, military organizations, and academic institutions. Here we are concerned not only with the effectiveness of the individual communication but with the role of communication in contributing to or detracting from the effective functioning of the total organization.

The nature of organizations is radically changing. For example, Kelley (1998) states:

> The old hierarchy is ending. Your company's future depends upon leadership, trust, and participation.

Greater emphasis than ever is being placed on "continuous improvement." In Japan, this is known as *kaizen* (*kai* means "change," and *zen* means "good" or "for the better") (Imai, 1986). An example of this is the story about several customers who are waiting in line for service (it could be anywhere). One person at the front of the line gets mediocre service, and everybody else gets mad. They say, "Who do you think you are, getting mediocre service—you are supposed to get lousy service like the rest of us!" This is just one indication of why organizations need to be striving toward *kaizen*.

Mass Communication

This last context involves *communication that is mediated*. That is, the source of a message communicates through some print or electronic medium. And mediated encounters differ from personal encounters (Avery and McCain, 1982). In addition, the message is intended for masses of individuals rather than for only a small number of individuals. Of the seven contexts of human communication discussed in this book, **mass communication** is the most formal—and the most expensive. Television advertisements during the Super Bowl each January will cost millions of dollars per minute! In addition, the opportunities for feedback are more limited, especially when compared with interpersonal or small-group communication. The audience in mass communication is relatively large, heterogeneous, and anonymous to the source. Finally, communication experience is characterized as public, rapid, and fleeting.

Bernard Goldberg states in his book *Bias* (2002) that in his many years as a television correspondent for CBS News, he noticed a systematic liberal bias in the coverage, not only in his network, but at ABC and NBC. He carefully documents numerous specific examples of this bias starting with the coverage of "conservative millionaire" Steve Forbes as a presidential candidate in 2000. If you are interested in this topic, you also would enjoy the opposing point of view expressed in the book by James Carvill and Paul Begala entitled *Buck Up, Suck Up . . . and Come Back When You Foul Up* (2002) Both of these are really great treatments of some of the issues regarding mass communication.

COMMUNICATION TECHNOLOGIES

We are all becoming increasingly familiar with what was once considered complex communication technology. For example, laptop computers have become a daily tool for many. Students walking across campus are often talking on their cell phones. Fax machines are so popular that fast-food restaurants like McDonald's use them to take orders.

Another technological wonder that has revolutionized human communication is the Internet. Although this has had positive effects, there have been some downsides too. One major study at Carnegie Mellon University (Harmon, 1998*) found that people who spend even a few hours a week on-line experience higher levels of depression and loneliness than people who use the computer less. The researchers concluded that Internet use itself appeared to cause a decline in psychological well-being. The study was funded by high-tech companies such as Hewlett-Packard, AT&T Research, Intel, Apple Computer, and the National Science Foundation, and the findings were exactly the opposite of what researchers were expecting to find. The researchers also concluded that the study "raises some troubling questions about the nature of 'virtual' communication and the disembodied relationships that are often formed in the vacuum of cyberspace" (p. A4).

*See Chapter 15 for more on the social effects of Internet use.

Another study looked into so-called Internet addiction (Lorek, 1998). How would you answer the questions below, using: 1, not at all; 2, rarely; 3, occasionally; 4, often; and 5, always.

Do you stay online longer than you intended?

Do you prefer the excitement of the Internet to the intimacy of your partner?

Do you check your e-mail before something else that you need to do?

Do you lose sleep at night due to late-night log-ons?

Do you choose to spend more time on-line than going out with others?

If you scored 5–9, you have average on-line use. If you scored 10–17, this would indicate some tendency toward Internet problems. If you scored 18–25, this would indicate some real tendency toward Internet problems. This is according to Kimberly Young at the University of Pittsburgh, who is co-founder of the Center for Online Addiction (p. 2E).

Even farmers have gone high tech. Kageyama (1992) reports that some farmers in Japan have outfitted their cattle with beepers. He reports that "he dials the cows' number on a portable phone to get their attention, and 'they look up immediately from eating the grass.' Usually they head for the feeding station, but sometimes they ignore the beeps and continue grazing" (p. A3).

With all this high-tech communication potential, human communication is at once more possible and perhaps less human. Regardless of your sentiments regarding these innovations, there is no question that they are having a profound and permanent impact on human communication.

Communication Ethics

This edition includes a chapter on ethics in communication. It seems that hardly a day goes by without some controversy being reported, whether it's deciding whether to clone human beings, or corporations abusing the environment, or Stanford University being accused of misusing overhead expense accounts from research grants. In any case, the chapter on communication ethics should provide you with some helpful insights and guidelines on how to avoid difficulties.

WHAT IS EFFECTIVE COMMUNICATION?

Earlier in this chapter we said that we would be concerned not only with human speech communication but with the concept of effective communication. But what are the criteria that make for effective communication? Students sometimes say that communication is effective when a person gets his or her point across. This is but one measure of effectiveness. More generally, communication is effective *when the stimulus as it was initiated and intended by the sender, or source, corresponds closely to the stimulus as it is perceived and responded to by the receiver.*

If we let *S* stand for the person who is the sender or source of the message and *R* for the receiver of the message, then communication is whole and complete when the response *S* intends and the response *R* provides are identical:

$$\frac{R}{S} = \frac{receiver's\ meaning}{sender's\ meaning} = 1$$

We rarely reach 1—that is perfect sharing of meaning. As a matter of fact, we never reach 1. We approximate it. And the greater the correspondence between our intention and the response we receive, the more effective we have been in communicating. At times, of course, we hit the zero mark: There is absolutely no correspondence between the response we want to produce and the one we receive. The drowning man who signals wildly for help to one of his friends on a sailboat only to have her wave back is not accomplishing his communication objective to say the least.

The example of the drowning man is extreme. By now you may be wondering just how important effective communication is on a day-to-day basis. A long-term study of Massachusetts Institute of Technology (MIT) graduates who were interviewed several times over a 15-year period has revealed that even for those very talented, technically competent people, graduates of a prestigious school, effectiveness in communication was one of the most important skills in achieving a successful and fulfilling life, if not the *most* important. On the basis of his research, the author of this study stresses the increasing importance of interpersonal competence as a skill critical "not only for dealing with self and family development, but for career advancement as well" (Schein, 1978, p. 77).

But how do we measure our own effectiveness? We can't judge our effectiveness if our intentions are not clear; we must know what we are trying to do. What makes that first definition of effectiveness inadequate ("when a person gets his or her point across") is that in communicating, we may try to bring about one or more of several possible outcomes. We shall consider five of them here: understanding, pleasure, attitude influence, improved relationships, and action.

Understanding

Understanding refers primarily to *accurate reception of the content of the intended stimulus.* In this sense, a communicator is said to be effective if the receiver has an accurate understanding of the message the communicator has tried to convey. (Of course, the communicator sometimes conveys messages unintentionally that are also quite clearly understood.)

The primary failures in communication are failures to achieve content accuracy. For example, the service manager of an oil company had a call one winter morning from a woman who complained that her oil burner was not working. "How high is your thermostat set?" he asked. "Just a moment," the woman replied. After several minutes she returned to the phone. "At 5 feet 3½ inches," she said, "same as it's always been." This confusion is typical of a failure to achieve understanding. Most misunderstandings of this kind are relatively easy to remedy through clarifying feedback and restatement.

As we add more people to a communication context, it becomes more difficult to determine how accurately messages are being received. This is one of the reasons that group discussions sometimes turn into free-for-alls. Comments begin to have little relation to one another, and even a group with an agenda to follow may not advance toward the resolution of any of its problems. Situations such as these call for more clarifying, summarizing, and directing of group comments.

With respect to public communication, much has been written about how to improve understanding when speaking to inform—with "understanding" often being referred to as "information gain." What the public speaker must remember is that the feedback he or she receives is often quite limited; the speaker should therefore make a concerted effort to be as objective and precise as possible in explaining his or her subject. The use of supporting materials—examples, analogies, and the like—helps clarify an explanation of almost any subject.

Within an organizational setting, accurate understanding is one of the most basic desired outcomes. It is not possible, for example, for an organization to function efficiently unless employees understand what they are expected to do at their jobs. This may involve understanding not only verbal directives from immediate superiors but also information disseminated through interoffice memos, employee handbooks, and other restatements of company policies.

In mass communication, the dissemination of information is also a primary objective on many occasions. (Newscasts, documentaries, and videotape programs immediately come to mind.) Presumably, those who work in the mass media have developed their communications skill to a high degree so that they are able to organize, present, and interpret information in a way that promotes understanding. For example, in a single hour a television special can present a program on depression: its symptoms, causes, and possible treatment. Because feedback is so limited in this setting, however, it is difficult to assess the level of information gain within the audience.

Pleasure

Not all communication has as its goal the transmission of a specific message. In fact, the goal of the transactional analysis school of thought is simply to communicate with others in a way that ensures a sense of mutual well-being. This is sometimes referred to as a **phatic communication,** or maintaining human contact. Many of our brief exchanges with others—"Hi"; "How are you today?"; "How's it going?" have this purpose. Casual dates, cocktail parties, and rap sessions are more structured occasions on which we come together to enjoy the company and conversation of others. (Some think that the word "rap" [as in Rap music] comes from the word "rapport," which refers to a positive relationship between people.) The degree to which we find communication pleasurable is closely related to our feelings about those with whom we are interacting. Recent research on cellular phone usage shows that the average U.S. teenager uses his or her cell phone 500 minutes a month, but 800 or 900 minutes per month is not unusual (LeDuc, 2001). See *dleduc@news-sentinel.com.*

The purpose of public communication can also be pleasure; the after-dinner speech and the speech intended to entertain fall into this category. Much of the informal communication within an organization takes place during lunch hours, coffee breaks, company picnics, and management club dances. And certainly in movies, situation comedies, and televised sports events, we see entertainment provided on a grand scale.

Attitude Influence

On August 23, 2001, former California Congressman Gary Condit appeared in a televised interview with ABC's Connie Chung in prime time to explain his relationship to his intern Chandra Levy who had been missing for 115 days. According to polls taken that night, 91 percent of those who watched said that they were not convinced by his statements. One representative source wrote, "Condit came across as robotic, scripted and unresponsive. He showed little compassion for the missing woman . . . In only one particular was he persuasive: He gave a convincing imitation of a politician whose career and reputation are toast" (McFeatters, 2001, p. 13A). It is hard to imagine a more ineffective attempt at influencing peoples' attitudes. Understanding and agreement are by no means synonymous outcomes. When you understand someone's message, you may find that you disagree with him or her even more strongly than you did before.

Influencing attitudes is a basic part of daily living. In many situations, we are interested in influencing a person's attitude as well as in having him or her understand what we are saying. The process of changing and reformulating attitudes, or **attitude influence,** goes on throughout our lives. In two-person situations, attitude influence is often referred to as "social influence." In the counseling interview, it might be called "gentle persuasion." Attitude influence is no less important in the small-group or the organizational setting. For example, consensus among group members is an objective of many problem-solving discussions. And industries often try, especially through the mass media, to influence public attitudes toward big business by presenting themselves in a flattering light. (For example, Exxon commercials about ecology suggest that the fuel industry is greatly concerned about the pollution problems caused by industrial waste.) When applied to public and mass communication contexts, the process of attitude influence is usually referred to as "persuasion." Studies of mass communication are particularly concerned with the persuasive impact of the message on various opinion leaders within the larger mass audience.

In determining how successful your attempts to communicate have been, remember that you may fail to change a person's attitude but still get that person to understand your point of view. In other words, a failure to change someone's point of view should not necessarily be written off as a failure to increase understanding.

Improved Relationships

It is commonly believed that if a person can select the right words, prepare his or her message ahead of time, and state it precisely, perfect communication will be ensured. But total effectiveness requires a positive and trusting psychological climate. When a human relationship is clouded by mistrust, numerous opportunities arise for distorting or discrediting even the most skillfully constructed messages. Voters may well be suspicious of their mayor's promise that if reelected, he will fulfill all the campaign promises he failed to keep during his first term in office. A young man will probably discount a young woman's assurances that she is very interested in him after she breaks a date for the third or fourth time. A professor may begin to doubt the excuses of a student who is holding court at the student union an hour after the student was too sick to take the midterm.

We mentioned that the primary failures in communication occur when the content of the message is not accurately understood. By contrast, secondary failures are disturbances in human relationships that result from misunderstandings. They stem from the frustration, anger, or confusion (sometimes all three) caused by the initial failure to understand. Because such failures tend to polarize the communicators involved, they are difficult to resolve. By acknowledging that the initial misunderstandings are a common occurrence in daily communication, we may be able to tolerate them better and avoid or at least minimize their damaging effect on interpersonal relationships.

Still another kind of understanding can have a profound effect on human relationships: understanding another person's motivations. At times each of us communicates not to convey information or to change someone's attitude but simply to be "understood" in this second sense. Throughout this text, we shall discuss various facets of human relationships: motivation; social choice; confirmation, self-disclosure, trust; group cohesiveness; and source credibility in public and mass communication. We hope to show that all these concepts are bound together by a common theme: The better the relationship between people, the more likely it is that other outcomes of effective communication in the fullest sense will occur.

Action

Some would argue that all communication is useless unless it brings about a desired action. Yet all the outcomes discussed thus far—understanding, pleasure, attitude influence, improved relationships—are important at different times and in different places. There are instances, however, when action is an essential determinant of the success of a communicative act. In the sales interview, an automobile salesman who wants you to think more favorably of his car than his competitor's also wants you to act by buying a car; his primary objective is not attitude change. A math tutor is far from satisfied if the student she is coaching says he understands how to do a set of problems but fails to demonstrate that understanding on his next exam. And we might question the effectiveness of a finance committee that reaches consensus on how to balance a budget yet fails to act on its decision.

Eliciting action on the part of another person is probably the communication outcome most difficult to produce. In the first place, it seems easier to get someone to understand your message than it is to get the person to agree with it. Furthermore, it seems easier to get that person to agree—that he or she should exercise regularly, for example—than to get the person to act on it. (We realize that some behaviors are induced through coercion, social pressure, or role prescriptions and do not necessarily require prior attitude change. Voluntary actions, however, usually follow rather than precede attitude changes.) If you are trying to promote action on the part of the receiver, you increase your chances of getting the desired response if you can (1) facilitate understanding of your request, (2) secure agreement that the request is legitimate, and (3) maintain a comfortable relationship with the receiver. The desired action does not follow automatically, but it is more likely to follow if these intermediate objectives have first been accomplished.

The difficulties of eliciting action on the part of the receiver are further compounded in organizational and mass communication settings. The plant manager's sharp memo on absenteeism, for example, may trigger more absenteeism, or the sick calls may taper off and some form of sabotage appear in the products turned out on the assembly line. Certainly, the mass media are often concerned with promoting audience action—whether it be promoting a particular brand of detergent, getting mothers to immunize their children against rubella, or changing audience voting patterns. Yet researchers have questioned the effectiveness of mass communication in changing behavior. It has been found, for example, that political campaigns conducted through the mass media have little direct influence on changes in voting behavior. One interesting new development intended to improve action as a result of communication is that the Federal Communications Commission has directed cell phone companies to start issuing phones that determine their locations through transmission towers or by global positioning satellites. In some cases, the accuracy must be within 150 feet. This is so that emergency crews can respond more quickly to urgent phone calls. However, it also raises the question of privacy, since all our calls can be traced to our sending location. You may want to discuss the pros and cons of this in your class (Kanaley, 2001).

In short, the five possible outcomes of effective human communication are understanding, pleasure, attitude influence, improved relationships, and action. At different points in this book, we shall give special attention to each of them. For example, the concepts of attitude similarity, status, social influence and consensus, and persuasion all have some bearing on attitude influence. Similarly, the concepts of trust, cohesiveness, and source credibility are all relevant to improved human relationships.

The five outcomes we have discussed are neither exhaustive nor mutually exclusive. Thus, a look at the relationship aspects of communication in Chapter 8 will illustrate that defensive behaviors distort understanding, that the so-called disconfirming responses are not pleasurable. In the chapters that follow, we hope to show some of the many ways in which communication outcomes are interdependent and to demonstrate that this is true for many different communication contexts, or settings.

Summary

In this book, we view human communication as the process of creating a meaning between two or more people. Today, many communication scholars emphasize the transactional nature of the communication process so that one person's communication can be defined only in relation to some other or others.

In this chapter, we presented a model to help us conceptualize the relationships between the elements of human communication. Like all human beings, both communicators in our model originate and perceive messages. Both depend on the steady flow of physical, social, and cultural input, and both select from the total input through their perceptual filters and sets.

We then discussed the components of a message in terms of the types of stimuli transmitted: verbal and nonverbal, intentional and unintentional. We learned that though all five senses are potential channels for receiving stimuli, face-to-face communication relies primarily on hearing, sight, and touch and is usually a multichannel experience. The channels of organizational communication would extend to newsletters, memos, and the like, whereas those of mass communication would include newspaper, films, radio, and television. Anything that distorts the information transmitted through the various channels or that distracts the receiver from getting it would be considered interference.

We saw that all the elements in Communicator 1's half of our communication cycle—input, filters, verbal and nonverbal messages, channels, and interference—are different for Communicator 2 because of his or her uniqueness as a human being. Emphasis was given to the receiver as listener. We examined the importance of feedback, and we examined the effect of time, represented in the model by a spiral, as a crucial variable in all studies of communication.

Much of the time people spend communicating involves interpersonal communication. But in studying human communication, we are also concerned with contexts in which a great many parties are involved, feedback is limited, and messages are transmitted through such media as newspaper, radio, and television. We are interested therefore in the principles of human communication as they apply not only to the two-person setting and the interview but to small-group, public, organizational, and mass communication. We are also interested in communication behaviors that are ethical.

After a brief discussion of each of the communication contexts, we turned to an examination of what constitutes effective communication. It was established that communication is effective to the degree that the message as it is intended by the sender corresponds with the message as it is perceived and responded to by the receiver. We learned that effectiveness is closely linked with intention and that in communicating, we usually want to bring about one or more of several possible outcomes. Five of the major outcomes—understanding, pleasure, attitude influence, improved relationships, and action—were considered here, with emphasis on their application to the various communication contexts. Another area of interest is intercultural communication, which cuts across all the contexts we shall be discussing.

Go to the Online Learning Center at www.mhhe.com/ tubbsmoss for glossary flashcards and crossword puzzles.

Key Terms

Communication	Input	Technical interference
Communication context	Messages	
Feedback	Semantic interference	

For further review, go to the Self-Quiz on the Online Learning Center at www.mhhe.com/ tubbsmoss.

Review Questions

1. Provide your own personal definition of "communication." How is it similar to, or different from, the definitions given in this text?

2. What is input, and how does it influence a person's communication?

3. Name the four types of messages. Give a specific example of each from your own experience.

4. Explain the difference between technical and semantic interference and give an example of each.

5. Discuss the influence of various kinds of feedback.

6. List seven different communication contexts. Explain the distinctive characteristics of each.

7. What is effective communication? Think of arguments for and against the types of communication effectiveness that have been described in this chapter. Are there some that the text has not included? Are there some it has discussed that you think should not be included? What do you think is the most important outcome of face-to-face communication?

Exercises

1. Start a personal log on the computer in which you record your daily reaction to perhaps ten members of your class. Only some will impress you (favorably or unfavorably) at first. Note details of their behavior. Describe your own responses as candidly as possible.

2. a. Draw and label a model of human communication. If possible, include components that can be appropriately labeled as Communicator 1 (sender/receiver), Communicator 2 (receiver/sender), input, filters, messages, channels, interference, and time.

b. Examine the model carefully and formulate five statements that describe how two or more components of the model may influence communication effectiveness as defined in this chapter.

3. Select a group of about ten students, and ask them to discuss one of the case problems listed in the appendix. The appendix can be found at *www.mhhe.com/tubbsmoss*. Observe the group and, if possible, tape-record the discussion. Analyze the group's communication in terms of intentional, unintentional, verbal, and nonverbal stimuli.

4. Write a short paper in which you analyze the strengths and weaknesses of the communication model in this chapter. Compare and contrast it with some other models, which may be found in the books in the suggested readings.

5. Divide the class members into groups of five or six; then have each group member discuss a personal problem in communication. Have each group select its "best" example of a communication problem as well as a spokesperson to present the example to the entire class. Then analyze each example in terms of the communication model given in this chapter.

6. Observe several communication events and keep a record of their outcomes. Which outcomes occurred most frequently? Under what conditions did these outcomes seem to occur? How can you explain these results?

7. Write a one-page case study of a communication failure that you have experienced or observed. Then write an analysis of its causes, and suggest a way to resolve it.

8. Think of two people you know, one an excellent communicator, the other quite ineffective. Write a highly specific description of each; then write a comparison of the two in which you contrast and evaluate their communication styles. On the basis of this analysis, set yourself three specific objectives for improving your own communication behaviors.

9. Check out the Internet for sources of information regarding communication.

Suggested Readings

Acuff, Frank L. *How to Negotiate Anything with Anyone Anywhere Around the World,* 2d ed. New York: American Management Association, 1997.

This excellent book helps explain how to apply communication principles in 41 countries. It is a very valuable resource.

Goldberg, Bernard. *Bias: A CBS Insider Exposes How the Media Distort the News.* Washington, D.C.: Regnery Publishing, 2002.

This best-selling book details a carefully researched account of the liberal bias in television news.

Gladwell, Malcolm. *The Tipping Point.* Boston: Little Brown and Company, 2000.

This best-selling book offers numerous principles and examples of communication in society.

O'Hair, Dan, and Lynda Dixon Shaver. *Strategic Communication,* 3d ed. Boston: Houghton Mifflin, 1998.

An interesting book that covers many topics related to this chapter.

Popcorn, Faith. *Clicking.* New York: HarperBusiness, 1998.

A remarkable view of life in the future. It has many implications for communication as our living patterns change.

Tapscott, Don. *Growing Up Digital: The Rise of the Net Generation.* New York: McGraw-Hill, 1998.

An excellent source of information about how the Internet is and will be used as a growing communication alternative at work, at play, and as a learning tool.

Trenholm, Sarah. *Thinking Through Communication,* 2d ed. Boston: Allyn and Bacon, 1998.

Intended for the advanced student, this book parallels many of the chapters in our book but at a purely theoretical level.

Person Perception

2

Chapter Objectives

After reading this chapter, you should be able to:

1. Explain the difference between a perceptual filter and a psychological set, and discuss the selective nature of all perception.
2. Describe how person perception differs from object perception and explain the implications of such differences for communication.
3. Discuss the development of self-concept and some of the variables that influence self-esteem, and state current research findings about self-esteem, shyness and Internet use, and the Pygmalion effect.
4. Describe the concepts of private personality theory, central traits, and primacy.
5. Discuss several variables, including perceived traits, physical attractiveness, and expressiveness, that influence our impressions of others.
6. Distinguish between personal generalizations and stereotypes, and discuss the effects of stereotyping.
7. Discuss how work, student, sex-linked, and marital roles influence person perception.
8. Describe several variables involved in forming accurate perceptions of others, and identify three ways to improve person perception and communication effectiveness.

It seems that we associate beauty with symmetry and are attracted by it. For example, in Western faces we know that average faces and symmetrical faces are regarded as attractive. A new study by Rhodes et al. (2001) looked at averageness and symmetry in Chinese and Japanese faces, using composite images that enhanced these qualities. The researchers found the same preferences and suggest that these standards of beauty may turn out to be biologically based.

Now take a careful look at the two faces in Figure 2.1, part of another intriguing crosscultural study of Caucasian and Japanese faces (Perrett et al., 1998). Examine the two female faces in the top half of Figure 2.1 and the two male faces below them. Which would you choose as ideal feminine and masculine faces?

The faces you see are computer composites—images blended to emphasize certain features, including face shape, associated with each sex. The woman's face at the upper left (masculinized at the right) has been feminized so that the bottom half of her face is narrower and her cheeks are higher and rounded. The man's face at the lower left has also been feminized, in contrast to the masculinized male image at the lower right, with its square face, enlarged jaw, and heavy brow. Researchers found that people of both sexes think that feminine features in both

Figure 2.1

Source: Perrett, D. I., K. J. Lee, I. Penton-Voak, et al., "Effects of Sexual Dimorphism on Facial Attractiveness," *Nature* 394 (August 27, 1998).

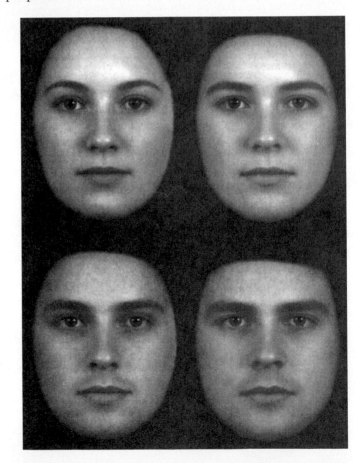

women and men are more attractive. This is true of both Caucasian and Japanese subjects. (Subjects also ranked the feminized male face with such traits as being more warm and more emotional, honest, and cooperative.)

What we judge to be attractive and how that perception affects our first impressions of others is just one of the many complex variables we will be looking at when we talk about person perception. Our impressions of others form the basis for numerous decisions throughout our lives not only in romantic relationships but in choosing one professor's course rather than another's, a roommate, a doctor, an advisor, or a business partner. In the following pages, we will be examining the initial process by which all such impressions of other human beings are formed.

PERCEIVING PEOPLE AND OBJECTS: A COMPARISON

Our total awareness of the world comes to us through our senses. Thus, all our perceptions—whether they be of drawings, household objects, or other people—have a common basis. Yet, as we've seen countless times, two people often disagree sharply in their judgments about a third. Have you ever been "fixed up" with someone described to you as just your type, only to be thoroughly disappointed from the very beginning of the evening? You might have even asked yourself whether the person who arranged the date perceived you or the other party with any accuracy. The reasons for such varying perceptions should become apparent as we consider similarities between interpersonal perception and perception in general.

Two Kinds of Filters

Your capacity to register sensory stimuli is limited. You cannot take in everything. Nor do you always want to. You choose certain aspects of your environment over others. What you are aware of at any time is determined in part by what you as a receiver select out of the total input. "You hear what you want to hear," mutters the irritated father to his teenage son, "This is the third time this afternoon I've asked you when you're going to get around to washing the car." Later that day, the same man may sit at the dinner table reading the Sunday paper, oblivious to a family quarrel that is taking place across the room. *The ability to process certain of the stimuli available to us while filtering out others* is called **selective attention**.

The American philosopher and psychologist William James explained the process of selection at work here in terms of interest: "Millions of items of the outward order are present to my senses which never properly enter into my experience. Why? Because they have no *interest* for me. *My experience is what I agree to attend to.* Only those items which I *notice* shape my mind—without selective interest, experience is an utter chaos" (James, 1950, p. 402).

Each of us, then, perceives only part of the available stimuli while filtering out other stimuli. There are two kinds of filters through which all input or sensation will pass: physiological and psychological.

Perceptual Filters and Psychological Sets

Among the inherent structures of our sense organs are our **perceptual filters,** *physiological limitations that are built into human beings* and cannot be reversed. Such limitations on our capacity to perceive exist whether we are experiencing an object or a person. And they vary considerably from one individual to another so that we differ in the degree to which our various senses are accurate.

To the human communicator one extremely troublesome perceptual filter is the limit on one's ability to hear. Sometimes we think we hear a person say one thing when actually he or she said another. We then act on the basis of what we think that person said. Or we may act without hearing what a person said at all. Many communication difficulties are rooted in this kind of misunderstanding. For example, one woman found out through a third party that she had antagonized her next-door neighbor by "cutting her dead." It turned out that the neighbor had walked by and said hello while the woman was standing at her front door anxiously awaiting her young son. This was the first day she had allowed him to walk home by himself from his first-grade class, and the boy was late. She was staring in the direction of the school and never even heard the neighbor's greeting. The neighbor, who was new to the community, interpreted the woman's unresponsiveness as a snub.

A psychological set is a second type of filter that influences our perceptions. Our **psychological sets**—that is, *our expectancies or predispositions to respond*—have a profound effect on our perception of objects. Similarly, psychological set affects our perception of other people. Suppose you were asked to interpret the scene pictured in Figure 2.2. How would you answer? Is the young woman sitting alone at the café because she is reading the piece of paper on the table? Is it a letter? If so, what does it say? Is she waiting for someone—or is she possibly attracted to the man at the next table? And why is he looking at her? An almost infinite number of interpretations can be evoked by an ambiguous illustration such as this one. Each of us has a story for this picture; with a little prodding, each of us could elaborate on it.

If you've had a disillusioning romantic relationship, you are more likely to perceive the young woman as lonely, perhaps reading a letter breaking off a relationship, because you've come to expect and anticipate such behavior. On the other hand, the piece of paper might be a menu. The man at the next table might be asking her for the time. Or perhaps he's even flirting. Whatever the story, it reveals much about your own expectations and past experiences. As you read on, you will see that past experience is a strong influence on what you select from all the available stimuli; and often you are judging another person, at least initially, by the group or context in which he or she is first seen. This will certainly be apparent when we discuss stereotyping.

Figure 2.2

Culture and Perception

One of the most powerful determinants of psychological set is culture. Consider the two parallel straight lines in Figure 2.3. Which would you say is longer? Chances are that if you live in a Western culture, you will perceive the bottom line as being the longer of the two. If you measure them, though, you will see that they are actually the same length. This is a well-known phenomenon called the *Müller-Lyer illusion*. It is an illusion in visual perception that Western peoples are particularly likely to experience and one to which certain non-Western peoples are much less susceptible.

   One explanation for the Müller-Lyer illusion is that people who live in a visual environment in which straight lines and right angles prevail—a "carpentered world" constructed with tools such as the saw, the plane, and the plumb bob—learn to make certain visual inferences. For example, they tend to interpret acute

Figure 2.3

and obtuse angles as right angles that are extended in space. This is what happens when Westerners look at Figure 2.3. From the two-dimensional drawing they make inferences about perspective, thus seeing the two lines as unequal in length. People who live in a culture that has very few structures made up of straight lines and corners—people from Ghana, for example—are not likely to experience the Müller-Lyer illusion because they do not tend to make such inferences about perspective (Segall et al., in Price-Williams, 1969). This is just one way in which culture influences our perception.

We have sets not only about objects and words but about other human beings—what they should look like, how they should act, and what they will say. In our culture, a business person expects people to be on time for appointments, and in turn those people do not expect to be kept waiting for long periods of time. When such expectancies are shared by all involved, they are often useful in facilitating communication. Other sets interfere with our ability to perceive accurately and respond appropriately. For example, some people—especially in telephone conversations—are so accustomed to being asked how they are that after saying "Hi" or "Hello," they answer "Fine" to whatever the other party has just said.

A great deal of interpersonal conflict stems from people's unawareness of the limits on their perceptual capacities. If they do realize the fallibility of their senses, they may be too defensive to acknowledge their mistakes. There is now convincing evidence that in some situations, if such a person is pressed, opposition to our point is likely to be reinforced instead of reversed, even though the person appears to be agreeing with us.

As two people communicate, each formulates ideas that become the content of the communication event. How accurately a message is received depends on the other person's perceptual filters and sets. Remember that psychological and physiological characteristics will influence which stimuli are selected and how they are perceived.

Selective Perception, Organization, and Interpretation

Today we don't believe, as early philosophers did, that the human mind is a blank tablet on which impressions are imprinted. We know that perception is not a passive state in which stimuli are received and automatically registered. Quite the opposite. Perception is an active process: Each of you *selectively* perceives, organizes, and interprets what you experience.

In general, you perceive stimuli that are intense, repetitious, or in the process of changing. Nonetheless, each person actively chooses what to attend to depending on personal interests, motivations, desires, and expectations.

Entranced by a young woman's appearance, a man sitting next to her at a party may notice what great legs she has and pay little attention to what she's saying. Someone else in the group may be more interested in her remarks about working in the personnel department of a large company because he is looking for a job.

In addition to the selective perception of stimuli, you tend to organize stimuli selectively—that is, you order the stimuli with which you are presented into a "whole," a complete, sensible picture. The test from which the ambiguous picture in Figure 2.2 derives is based on this notion.

People organize stimuli according to different schema and expectations: they attribute cause and effect uniquely. A quarrel between husband and wife in which he claims to withdraw because she nags while she claims to nag because he withdraws is such an example: The differences in organizing the sequence are at the heart of their different perceptions. Asked to explain, the husband maintains his withdrawal is his sole defense against his wife's nagging. She, in turn, sees his explanation as a deliberate distortion of "what 'really' happens"—that the reason for her critical attitude is the husband's passivity (Watzlawick et al., 1967, pp. 56–57).

After stimuli are selectively perceived and selectively organized, they are selectively interpreted—that is, the stimuli are assigned meanings unique to the perceiver. Personal interpretations are based on the perceiver's past experiences, assumptions about human behavior, knowledge of the other's circumstances, present moods/wants/desires, and expectations.

Perceiver/Object/Context

Like perceiving objects, perceiving other people may be thought of in terms of three elements: the perceiver, the object of perception (in this instance, another human being), and the context within which the object is viewed. As the perceiver, you are of course influenced by your own attributes. For example, people seem to have predispositions to make generally negative or positive evaluations of others; certainly we have all met someone who feels that "people are no damn good" or, at the other end of the spectrum, someone who would say that there's good to be found in all of us. It is through the eyes of the perceiver that all the attributes of that second person (the object, if you will) are filtered. Remember, though, that because person perception is a transactional process, those attributes do not always remain constant. If early in our first conversation you act as if I'm a terrible bore, you might find that my behavior changes from mildly friendly to just plain obnoxious. As for the third element, the context or setting within which the process of interpersonal perception occurs is both physical and psychological, as we shall see.

To some degree, however slight, we assume that the other person shares some of our characteristics, that we resemble each other in some ways. We are—or so we think—familiar with some of the other person's experience. Such assumptions may help us perceive more accurately. For example, if I know that you have just returned from a funeral, on the basis of my own experiences I will probably interpret your silence as depression rather than indifference. On the other hand, we often misinterpret what we perceive precisely because we assume other people are like us. If I assume that your taste in music is like mine, when I offer to play some country music, I may interpret your remark "Oh, great!" as genuinely enthusiastic though it is clear to most people from your facial expression that your reply was sarcastic.

Another way in which perceiving people differs from perceiving objects is that our perceptions and misperceptions influence and keep on influencing our interactions with others—because they keep responding to these perceptions. Sometimes people correct our misperceptions. But occasionally one misinterpretation leads to another, and we get further and further afield.

Person perception then is a special form of perception. As we go on to examine how impressions of others are formed, we will also give some attention to how members of other cultures tend to be perceived.

FORMING IMPRESSIONS

Our concern with the process of forming impressions involves the discussion of many variables, but it begins with you, the perceiver, and how you view yourself.

Looking at Yourself

If asked to describe yourself, what information would you give—a physical description, your age, gender, membership in an ethnic group? Perhaps you would define yourself by certain traits or by what you do. You might say you are a student, that you are outgoing and interested in politics, or that you are athletic and somewhat shy. For some, self-description is an uncomfortable process. For example, one college application asks prospective students to describe themselves by using ten adjectives. One reason college applications can be so difficult to fill out is that they often require statements about self-concept.

Self-Concept

Your **self-concept,** *your relatively stable impressions of yourself,* includes not only your perception of your physical characteristics but your judgments about what you "have been, are, and aspire to be" (Pearson et al., 1995). Self-concept develops partly out of the feedback you receive from the people around you. In fact, some early theorists believe that there is a "**looking glass self**" that develops out of our relations and interactions with others. In other words, you evaluate yourself primarily on the basis of how you *think* others perceive and evaluate you. You combine all these reflected perceptions, ways in which you think others see you, and they make up what Mead (1934) calls "the generalized other."

Such a view gives great weight to your experiences as a child. If, for example, Maria's parents, relatives, and school friends all come to think of her as "the good student," she may learn to regard herself in the same way and strive even harder to do well in classes. Academic performance may become an essential aspect of the way she thinks of herself. Conversely, if Jermaine is viewed by his parents, relatives, and neighbors as "the black sheep," he may come to see himself in this light.

Self-concept not only grows out of your social interactions but changes with your age as well as your situation—for example, you might see yourself very differently when at home than you do when you are away at college (Hinde et al., 2001, p. 190). Self-concept can vary so much with context that some suggest viewing the self "not as a unitary structure, but as multiple." It's been proposed also that different people who know us know different aspects of the self. "And the self must be seen as an active agent, providing expectancies and directing attention to whatever is of significance to the individual" (pp. 190–191).

Self-concept also has a comparative dimension. For example, Kagan writes: "Although a particular child is a female, Canadian, Catholic, with brown eyes, she is also prettier than her sister, smarter than her best friend, and more fearful of animals than her brother" (1989, p. 244). So a good part of how you think about yourself may have to do with how you judge yourself in relation to others.

Self-Esteem

One of the chief measures of self-concept is **self-esteem,** *your feelings of self-worth.* Your self-esteem might be linked with your physical appearance, intelligence, work, any number of qualities, traits, and affiliations, but self-esteem may be entirely subjective. Current research indicates that "self-esteem is not in and of itself a strong predictor of success" (Johnson, 1998). There may be no direct relationship between your actual traits, achievement, or competence, and your feelings of self-worth (Sternberg and Kolligian, 1990). For example, a study of 1000 women who achieved considerable success in their careers finds that many described themselves as "shy," "sensitive," and "self-critical" (Rimm, 1999, p. 8). Other research on exceptionally bright students shows that academic excellence does not necessarily make for high self-esteem. One high-achieving college student recalls:

> Everyone in 7th grade hated me, with some exceptions. My friends were the "out" class. The popular kids looked down on me. I felt dirty, unclassy, unfeminine. It was worse in 8th. The one thing my ego was based on was being smart. (Janos, 1990, p. 108)

Many studies of children report differences in self-esteem between boys and girls. In general, boys have a tendency "to inflate their sense of competence" while girls usually play down their own abilities. Traditionally, our culture has handed down different behavioral norms and role models for male and female children. Consider this example:

> A boy in a mass communication research project is asked what he would like to be when he grows up if he were a girl. "Oh," he exclaimed, "if I were a girl, I'd have to grow up to be nothing." (Lazier-Smith, 1989, p. 247)

Current research suggests that such patterns are cultural and conveyed through what parents believe and expect concerning their children's capabilities (Bandura, 1990, pp. 344–345). For example, studies by Gilligan and others (1982; 1989) propose that because most women are brought up to emphasize caring and responsibility for others rather than autonomy and independence, they tend to develop different moral value systems than men.

A summary of research on self-esteem (Pearson et al., 1995) includes these differences between men and women:

- Men have a higher expected success rate on nonsocial skills than do women; even when men do not perform better, people perceive that they do.
- Single women have higher self-esteem than do married women.
- Older children score higher on self-esteem than do younger children.
- Similarity in self-esteem appears to be a factor in selecting someone to date or have a relationship [with].

Linked as it is with individualism, self-esteem is often highly regarded in the United States, but it's not only some high achievers who have high self-esteem—so do gang members and violent criminals. Indeed, "aggressive, violent, and hostile people consistently express favorable views of themselves" and when those views are threated, the potential for violence is unleashed if the person in question is unstable or has an inflated sense of self (Baumeister et al., 1999). A recent survey of self-esteem research (Baumeister, 1998) summarizes the findings:

> First, high self-esteem is linked to various positive outcomes and low self-esteem to bad outcomes, but often the self-esteem is the result rather than the cause. Second, high self-esteem does seem to make people feel better, and so it is subjectively pleasant. Third, high self-esteem has a small number of practical material benefits, such as greater persistence in the face of failure. Fourth, most social and personal problems are not caused by a lack of self-esteem, so raising self-esteem is unlikely to solve them. Fifth, high self-esteem, especially when not grounded in actual accomplishments, may breed interpersonal violence and other possible undesirable consequences. (p. 699)

In another new study Schütz (2001) found that high self-esteem, though it has many benefits, can sometimes be disruptive socially, fostering a negative attitude toward other human beings. Certain interpersonal strategies for presenting yourself can also put down other people. For example:

> Presenting yourself positively while criticizing others.
>
> Overemphasizing your own abilities and devaluing those of other people.
>
> Overestimating your own attractiveness and minimizing your responsibilities for social conflicts. (Adapted from p. 172)

It seems, then, that high self-esteem is not always a predictor of positive attitudes toward others.

Feedback

Feedback often has a direct effect on level of self-esteem. When people are asked to predict their own performance on a test—whether it be of social, intellectual, or physical competence—and are later given feedback on how well they scored, they revise their predictions for the next experimental task in the direction of that feedback. This is true regardless of whether the feedback is accurate or not.

Numerous studies of speech communication feedback suggest that this commonsense hunch is correct: When you get positive feedback, you gain in self-confidence. Negative feedback can make you flustered and cause disruptions in your delivery, whether this is indicated by the loudness of your voice, rate of speech fluency, nervousness, stage fright, eye contact, or body movement.

Current research on how we *perceive* our own abilities supports the view that our relationships with others make up the foundation out of which we develop a sense of self and competence (Schaffer and Blatt, 1990, p. 244). Some researchers believe that earlier theories about self-concept are still useful as a base for further studies on how the self develops in social contexts (Hinde et al., 2001; May, 1991).

There seem to be some gender differences with respect to feedback. Because women tend to give more importance to how others evaluate them, research has found, "women were more likely to consider . . . feedback accurate and to take it seriously (unrelated to any differences in self-confidence)—in other words, feedback had more information value for women than for men" (Deaux and LaFrance, 1998, p. 810). For example, the effect of negative stereotyping by employers would seem to influence a woman's evaluation of herself more than it would a man's self-evaluation.

Shyness

"Do you consider yourself to be a shy person?" This is one of the questions with which Zimbardo began his pioneering studies of shyness over twenty-five years ago. According to Zimbardo, "the average person you meet is either shy, used to be shy, or is easily shy in certain situations." In fact, "only about 10 percent of Americans say they've never felt shy" (Kutner, 1992; Jones et al., 1986; Zimbardo, 1990).

Today much is known about shyness. For example, researchers have found that some people have a "temperamental bias," or genetic predisposition, toward shyness; interestingly enough, this includes some physical traits such as light-colored eyes. Shyness has many physical symptoms, and these vary from one person to another—trembling, rapid heartbeat, dry mouth, sweating, blushing. Shy people date less frequently, have fewer friends, "tend to have low-esteem and are preoccupied with the thought that they are socially inadequate" (Cheek and Cheek, 1990, p. 15).

We take for granted our sense of self. If you have been raised in a Western culture, you probably tend to see yourself as independent of others—you make choices, decide for yourself, and feel relatively autonomous. Yet theorists are finding that there may be great cultural variation in self-concept—that is, in how the self is conceived. Western culture tends to promote *an independent self* that values self-direction, personal self-esteem and achievement, and freedom in relationships. Other cultures, including those from East Asia, seem to promote *an interdependent self* that places highest value on connection, collective self-esteem, and group achievements, being part of the ingroup (Ting-Toomey, 1999, p. 29).

Thus, a recent study of U.S. and Japanese students finds the Japanese more responsive to situation and self-critical (Kanagawa et al., 2001). For example, to someone Japanese describing yourself as kind or attractive might not be appropriate because that judgment should be made by the person you are with (p. 101). While American culture encourages developing "an independent view of the self—to be unique, to express the self, and to realize [your] own thoughts, feelings, and capacities," Kanagawa finds the Japanese emphasize their similarity to others and how they fit into different social situations (p. 99).

Like Japanese culture, Chinese culture seems to foster an interdependent self. The emphasis in Confucianism is on relatedness to others—often in a hierarchical relationship. In Chinese, for example, there is no word for brother. Instead, there is one word for older brother and a different word for younger brother.

"For the Chinese," writes Stella Ting-Toomey, "the 'self' is both a center of relationships and a dynamic process of development within a network of relationships. In Chinese culture, to be aware of one's relations with others is an integral part of *zuo ren,* or 'conducting oneself properly' in getting along with others . . . Chinese can never separate themselves from obligations to others and Chinese sense of self-worth is closely tied with kinship and social networks" (Ting-Toomey, 1999, p. 78).

What has shaped your own self-concept? Do you think of yourself as more independent or more connected with others?

Because they have lower self-esteem, they also tend to apply for jobs beneath their level of skills and to settle for the first job offer that comes along. In general, they earn less and advance less in their work because, as researchers explain, "shy people self-select themselves out of high-paying careers" (Cheek and Cheek, 1990, p. 176).

Now new studies suggest that in some situations shy people can overcome their reticence. In making the transition to the social setting of the university, first-year students enter a new social setting that is unfamiliar to them. They are also in a setting in which they are evaluated on an ongoing basis: professors are evaluating their intellectual capacities; and other students, most of whom are strangers, are evaluating their "intellectual, social, and sexual attractiveness." Certainly, this is a time in life that one would expect to intensify feelings of shyness. Yet in a study of students at Berlin University, Asendorpf (2000) found that leaving home to start at the university was apparently not threatening to shy students. And although it took more time for shy students to expand their social network of peers, they too forged new relationships. For shy students a major difference seemed to be that a considerable number were often lonely, and while other first-year students described themselves as in love "at any point in time," this was true of only a third of shy students. Then too even when love and support were present in their relationships, shy students tended to feel more loneliness than students who are not shy.

More encouraging results come from several studies on the effects of technology use—specifically, use of the computer to access the Internet. It seems that there is considerable evidence that shy people reduce their levels of shyness online and that sometimes as a result of online successes they then reduce levels of shyness offline (Roberts et al., 2000).

A growing body of research and case material shows that shyness is sometimes outgrown and that it is treatable. You can find out more about approaches to treatment of shyness and a new study on social interaction and technology at *www.shyness.com.*

Self-Fulfilling Prophecies

For artists, writers, and scientists, early rejection has usually been "the rule rather than the exception"—the careers of architect Frank Lloyd Wright, dancer Martha Graham, sculptor Louise Nevelson, and novelist James Joyce offer just a few examples. We know that people who have the same set of skills "can perform poorly, adequately, or extraordinarily" and that often one's sense of competence and self-esteem can contribute to success (Bandura, 1990, p. 315).

Our expectations also have an influence on our impressions of other people. People who expect to be accepted by others and who perceive others as friendly are often outgoing and congenial; and their behavior accounts in good measure for their popularity and the positive way in which others respond. On the other hand, people who expect to be rejected often are (Adelmann, 1988). Perceiving others as hostile or unfriendly, they often act defensive or superior; this behavior may very well set in motion the rejection they fear. And a person who thinks his relationship with someone is casual rather than exclusive may therefore spend little time with the other person so that indeed the relationship never deepens (Honeycutt and Cantrill, 2001, p. 166).

Because of their psychological set, these people help to confirm their own expectations so that a favorable self-concept may lead to success, an unfavorable self-concept to failure. This phenomenon is called a **self-fulfilling prophecy.**

A Greek myth tells the story of Pygmalion, a young sculptor who created an exquisite ivory statue of a beautiful woman and fell in love with it. Pygmalion prayed to Aphrodite, the goddess of love, that the statue might come to life, and the ivory figure became flesh and moved on her pedestal. Pygmalion named her Galatea, and the two were married in the presence of Aphrodite.

In a much-discussed experiment, Rosenthal and others studied what came to be known as the **Pygmalion effect,** *a self-fulfilling prophecy in which "one person's expectation for another person's behavior can quite unwittingly become a more accurate prediction for its having been made"* (Rosenthal and Jacobson, 1992, p. vii, emphasis added). Essentially, Rosenthal's study found that when, at the beginning of the school year, elementary school teachers were given information that led them to believe certain pupils ranked higher than others in intellectual competence (supposedly measured by IQ tests), those "special" children showed dramatic intellectual growth and ranked far above the "ordinary" children. The results have been interpreted in many ways. Rosenthal speculates that

> by what she said, by how and when she said it, but [also by] her facial expressions, postures, and perhaps by her touch, the teacher may have communicated to children of the experimental group that she expected improved intellectual performance. Such communications together with possible changes in teaching techniques may have helped the child learn by changing his self-concept, his expectations of his own behavior, and his motivation, as well as his cognitive style and skills. (p. 180)

A striking example of self-fulfilling prophecy, the Pygmalion effect has been observed in educational, medical, and many other contexts.

Behavior Attribution

There seems to be a major difference between the way you perceive yourself and the way you perceive others. A series of studies on **behavior attribution** suggests that *you see your own behavior as a sequence of responses to the demands of a given situation, but you view the same behavior in others as generated by their disposition,* that is, their stable traits or needs. Lee, for example, sees himself as cutting down on his expenses and living more economically because he's saving up for a car; but he tends to think of Adam, his roommate, as cheap. Or "She is arrogant," but "I was provoked." In addition, a consistent finding in attribution research is that we tend to attribute the causes of our success to ourselves and the causes of our failures to external factors (Nurmi, 1991).

Two reasons for these perceptual differences have been proposed. First, the information available to the actor (the one who performs the action) and the observer may be different. The observer sees the actor at a particular point in time. Generally, he or she does not—cannot—know firsthand the actor's history, experiences, motives, or present emotional state; these can only be inferred. Thus, if we see a person overreact to a mildly critical remark, as observers, we may not know what events preceding this episode made it the straw that broke the camel's back. A second possibility is that even when the same information is available to both actor and observer, they process it differently because different aspects of it are salient to each of them.

These information differences may exist in actor and observer because their points of view are literally quite different. You do not see yourself acting; under ordinary circumstances you cannot be an observer of your own behavior. And while as an actor you watch the situation in which you find yourself, the other person spends most of his or her time observing you, not the situation (Storms, 1973). One recent study (Hancock and Dunham, 2001) found that the impressions people formed during *computer-mediated communications* (**CMC**) are less detailed than they are in face-to-face settings but personality attributions are more intense and extreme. Earlier studies had shown no differences.

Suppose we reverse the viewpoints of actor and observer. Storms found that he could change the orientation of actor and observer by showing them videotapes of their own interaction. Videotape offered the actor a new perspective, that of an observer, and often changed his or her inferences about why he or she had behaved in a particular way. After seeing ourselves on tape, we are much more likely to explain our behavior as a reflection of personal disposition than as a response to the environment.

While a change in visual orientation seems to heighten self-awareness, the prospect of viewing videotapes of all our behavior is neither appealing nor feasible. Nor is it perhaps desirable. Storms mentions, for example, that when videotape is used in therapy, patients sometimes take undue responsibility for their behavior, overlooking genuine elements in the environment that have influenced their actions. Videotape is not the answer. What we need is a more balanced view of ourselves and of others, a view that enables us to interpret behavior in terms of both disposition and environment.

Research on behavior attribution has several implications. The most important for our purposes is that by combining information about ourselves that is available only to us with an awareness of how other human beings perceive us, we may begin to see ourselves in sharper perspective.

Looking at Others

In many situations, we find ourselves making several judgments about others—and all at once. For example, Matt Philips was at a Christmas party. Mixed in with the old crowd were four people he didn't know. But by the end of the evening he had, at least to his own satisfaction, sized up all the newcomers. The young woman in the red dress was lively and pleasant; he liked her right away. But her husband was a terrible snob—and so self-involved. The tall blonde was too nervous, but the older man seated next to her was easygoing with a great sense of humor. And Matt noticed how confident he was—they spent quite a bit of time talking.

Like Matt, most of us form impressions of others quite easily; yet we find it difficult to explain the process. In fact, many feel that they make their judgments intuitively. One study of dating found "that dates are rapidly defined as promising or not (in the first 30 seconds!)" (cited in Duck, 1992).

In one study of how people form impressions of others in cyberspace, Jacobson (1999) looked at online expectations and offline experiences in text-based virtual communities called MOOs. One woman explained how she perceived the difference:

> On MOO everything can seem larger than life—it can be quite a surprise to realize the people are ordinary. People here can seem more witty and amusing and clever and sexy than the people one knows irl [in real life]. People project a persona here sometimes, and when you meet them they are shyer or whatever. A friend of mine said he was disappointed when he first started meeting people from the MOO. He had the impression they were demi-gods. (p. 12)

"Impression" is a word we use about our judgments. We speak of being "under the impression," or of someone making a "lasting impression," a "false impression," or a "good impression." Even our legal system reflects the degree to which we rely on snap judgments. Before a trial begins, prospective jurors are screened by the defense and the prosecution. In addition to raising specific objections to certain candidates for the jury, both the defense and the prosecuting attorneys are allowed to reject a certain number of would-be jurors without stating their reasons. Attorneys often make their decisions rapidly, though they are complex ones and are probably based on several considerations. They will probably take into account their perception of the potential juror and the client and the impression they feel that the client will make upon that juror. And, of course, the attorney for one side might be more than willing to accept a juror whom opposing counsel finds objectionable.

Attorneys usually seem to be rather skilled perceivers, accustomed to formulating judgments about others very quickly. But think of the members of the jury. They will be meeting and evaluating many people for the first time and presumably doing this entirely on their own. In a short time each juror will probably have formed an impression of most if not all of those involved in the case—including the witnesses, the defense attorney, the prosecuting attorney, and even the judge.

Research on person perception in legal settings confirms that a juror's perception of an attorney's credibility and of the defendant's guilt will be influenced not only by the attorney's opening statements but by various nonverbal cues in delivering those statements.

Because a juror's final judgment about the person on trial can have dramatic consequences, it is important to consider how he or she forms initial impressions and whether those impressions will have any effect on later perceptions. Our own evaluations of people also have important if less dramatic consequences, so we might all benefit from looking more closely at how an impression of another person is formed.

The First Impression

One of the major uses of evaluating personality is to explain and predict behavior on the basis of very limited information. How do we put this information together and come up with a first impression? Actually, each of us seems to hold a **private theory of personality** (sometimes known as "implicit personality theory"). Essentially, the term refers to *how we select and organize information about other people on the basis of what behaviors we think go together.*

Suppose you are given the following list of words describing a man you have never met and are then asked to write a personality sketch of him:

energetic	ironical
assured	inquisitive
talkative	persuasive
cold	

In a classic experiment, Solomon Asch (1946) used this list to learn more about how impressions of others are formed. He read the list to a group of students and asked them to write a full impression of the person described by these adjectives. There were two important findings.

Unity   Asch's first finding was unity. All the students were able to organize the scanty information they received and create a consistent, unified impression, though there was a great deal of variation in their personality sketches, and they all went beyond the terms of the original description. Here are two samples:

> He seems to be the kind of person who would make a great impression upon others at a first meeting. However, as time went by, his acquaintances would easily come to see through the mask. Underneath would be revealed his arrogance and selfishness.

> Possibly he does not have any deep feeling. He would tend to be an opportunist. Likely to succeed in things he intends to do. He has perhaps married a wife who would help him in his purpose. He tends to be skeptical. (Asch, 1946, p. 261)

Central Traits   Second, Asch found that certain traits are more *central,* more influential than others in forming impressions of personality. When one of the adjectives on the list was replaced by its opposite, the personality descriptions were radically different. Whether a person is warm or cold was more important than whether he is blunt or polite.

Do we like people who argue less? A study of argumentative situations (Onyekwere et al., 1991) reports that those who rank higher in argumentativeness and are more committed or attached to the issue being debated are perceived more positively than those who argue less and are less committed to the topic. When highly argumentative subjects were less involved about issues they were debating, they were viewed less favorably, so it appears that being partisan is significant. In essence, the researchers speculate, "when people like what they are doing, they may be perceived as more trustworthy because their enthusiasm, excitement and confidence may be interpreted as more sincere and dependable behaviors" (p. 45).

For a long time, theorists believed that impressions of others were interpreted on the basis of the *halo effect,* the tendency to extend a favorable or unfavorable impression of one trait to other traits. Thus, you might think of Donna as honest and polite, just because you consider her intelligent. Or if you feel Paul is cheap, you might attribute several other undesirable traits to him. This explanation sounds reasonable, but we now know that the halo effect is too simple a concept to account completely for the way we interpret our perceptions.

Indirectly, experiments tell us that certain traits carry weight and are clearly more decisive in our judgments than others. Somehow we manage to make all the information we have about a person—all those distinct verbal and nonverbal cues—fit together (Asch and Zukier, 1984; Bruner, 1986). If they don't seem consistent, we build in an explanation.

People seem more reliable, more knowable, when we can predict some aspects of their behavior. Perhaps that explains our need to perceive another human being as a "personality"—to see that personality quickly; to see it vividly, with certain dominant or central traits; and most important, to see it as a unity.

The Primacy Effect

Time is one of the most significant variables in our communication model. Thus, it seems natural to ask what effect the first impression you form will have on your later perceptions of another person. Ideally, as you learn more about someone, you continually revise or refine your impressions in the light of new information. But is this in fact so? Does a first impression enhance or interfere with later knowledge, or does it have no effect at all?

Among early studies of impression formation, those of Luchins have been very influential. In one of Luchins's experiments, subjects read two paragraphs describing a young man named Jim. One paragraph described actions of Jim's that were predominantly introverted, the other described actions that were predominantly extroverted. All subjects read the same paragraphs; only their order varied. Luchins found that a **primacy effect** did exist—that *the first information we receive about a person is the most decisive in forming our impression* (Luchins, in Hovland et al., 1957). So first meetings—especially the very first minutes of those meetings—are important.

Primacy has a clear-cut effect on communication. If you look once more at the model in Figure 1.1 (page 9), you can see that each communicator should be receiving input and feedback. The primacy effect blocks both. It is, in our terms, a source of technical interference, and this time the interference is within the communicator. If Sandra, after spending five minutes with her roommate's brother Bill, is sure that he is overbearing and phony, she is not going to be very interested in getting any feedback about her impression of him. Most of you have been in Bill's place at least once. It's as though you suddenly had become invisible. No matter what you said or did, the other person no longer seemed to respond; you couldn't change that first impression of you.

Rightly or wrongly, most people feel quite confident about their judgments. For example, in Luchins's experiment almost all the subjects were very willing to answer questions about Jim's behavior that were totally unrelated to the information they had read about him. Given information about some of his behavior, they inferred several other things about him and confidently predicted how he would behave in other social situations. Only a few asked how they were expected to know such things (Brown, 1986). But as we will see in Chapter 3, all inferences involve some measure of risk, and this is true of inferences about personality.

We all know how often first impressions can be mistaken ones, and we also know how often decisions depend on first impressions. Imagine that you are being interviewed for your first job after graduation. You look very nervous and were 10 minutes late for the interview. Then you make an obvious grammatical mistake in speaking. What is likely to be the outcome?

It's disturbing to think that first impressions can have such dramatic effects on judgment. But Luchins found that if people were warned not to make snap judgments, the primacy effect was reversed or eliminated completely. Several other studies confirm that the primacy effect is not inevitable.

Physical Attractiveness

In some ideal world we will all be beautiful. Until that time, however, it seems likely that those of us who are physically attractive will have a slight edge—at least initially—on those of us who are not. Among scholars there is general agreement: Physically attractive people are considered by others to be more sociable, more popular, more sexual, more successful, and more persuasive. And frequently they are thought to be happier and to have more appealing personalities (Berscheid and Reis, 1998).

As we saw at the beginning of this chapter, some standards of beauty may be universal. Other aspects of attractiveness seem to be influenced by culture. For example, in our own culture being attractive is often associated with thinness, so that one of the unpardonable sins—at least for women—is becoming "fat." Witness the alarming number of women suffering from such eating disorders as anorexia and bulimia: As many as 22 percent of college women may be affected (Gustafson et al., 2001). The National Eating Disorders Association reports that every day thousands of people log on to Internet clubs and websites that discuss and advise about weight loss and that ultimately promote eating disorders ("Anorexia's Web," 2001).

We take many of our images of beauty from the mass media, yet consider the following statistics:

- The average American woman is 5′4″ tall and weights 140 pounds.
- 80 percent of American women are dissatisfied with their appearance.
- The average American model is 5′11″ tall and weights 117 pounds.
- Most fashion models are thinner than 98 percent of American women. *(www.edap.org)*

Many studies of body images that appear in women's magazines confirm what most of us already know: that ads do not represent a diversity of body types. Instead they promote the stereotype of a "thin ideal" which has become a social and cultural norm, associated not only with beauty but success (Gustafson et al., 2001).

Recently there has been a great surge in the popularity of dating services and the number of people placing personal ads in newspapers and magazines. Duck (1992) notes the finding that "men 'offer' their status and height when describing themselves, while women 'offer' physical attractiveness."

Aside from liking physically attractive people because they are good to look at, we sometimes like them because we feel that by being seen with them, we will enhance our own image. The college man who consistently dates beautiful women is very likely to improve his own image among both his male friends and his prospective female acquaintances. The woman who dates handsome men is also increasing her own self-esteem. One article described arrangements in which a man or woman seeks a good-looking escort for an evening out, "arm candy":

> implying a beautiful object to attach to your arm, for others to feast their eyes upon. In the image-obsessed 1990s, when a dominant mood is the desire to inspire fits of envy in one's friends, a woman (and sometimes a man) in the role of arm candy expresses the quintessential modern relationship. (Kuczynski, 1998, sec. 9, p. 1)

Attractiveness may also be linked with perceptions of power and status. One study reveals that American women perceive men dressed in formal attire as more attractive than men who are informally dressed (Hewitt and German, 1987).

It also turns out that subjects differing in their levels of attractiveness are distinguishable on the basis of their attitudes toward relationships (Erwin and Calev, 1984). Attractive subjects viewed their friendships in terms of personal rewards and being liberal and "easygoing"; those of average attractiveness viewed them in terms of personal reward and involving commitment; unattractive subjects emphasized social and commitment aspects of their relationships. The authors of the study believe their findings may support the matching hypothesis—people of like levels of attractiveness stay together because like levels of attractiveness may reflect similar attitudes toward friendship.

Despite the association of beauty with talent, however, career success for women is not furthered by their good looks. In fact, studies point to a bias against good-looking women in managerial and executive positions (Zebrowitz, 1997). Attractive women who run for public office, unlike their male counterparts, also seem to be at a disadvantage. The so-called beauty backlash applies only to women.

In general, researchers tend to agree that the influence of physical beauty is most powerful early in a relationship (Knapp and Vangelisti, 2000). As we acquire more and more information about a person, the effects of physical appearance diminish considerably. It seems, after all, that you can't "live on looks."

Expressiveness

One of the great problems Al Gore had during his campaign for president in 2000 was that he appeared "wooden." This stiffness and seeming lack of spontaneity was quite apparent during his debates with George W. Bush. Today there is a growing body of research about expressiveness and charisma. According to recent findings, **expressiveness,** *a dimension of nonverbal communication that influences our first impressions, has been linked with animation, dynamism, expansiveness, and intensity of both nonverbal and verbal behaviors* (DePaulo and Friedman, 1998). It seems to include elements of extraversion but to incorporate many other behaviors: "Expressiveness (or 'spontaneous sending') is often construed as the ease with which people's feelings can be read from their nonverbal expressive behaviors when they are not deliberately trying to communicate their feelings to others" (p. 13).

Expressiveness also seems to reflect physical well-being. People who are considered more expressive usually attract more attention, and we usually think of them as more attractive. They tend to create first impressions that are extremely favorable, and such impressions tend to be sustained over time:

> [E]xpressiveness makes one seem more attractive, as does one's ability to regulate nonverbal behaviors in ways that are appealing . . . Studies of personal charisma, which examine both fixed attractiveness and expressiveness, suggest that expressiveness is at least as important as physical attractiveness—perhaps even more so—in account[ing] for immediately favorable first impressions. Many charismatic actors would be judged plain and unappealing from photographs alone; conversely, one's perceptions of a striking beauty can be obliterated by the first few minutes of a conversation. (DePaulo and Friedman, 1998, pp. 13–14)

Personal Generalizations and Stereotypes

For good or ill, your private theory of personality is in large part based on generalizations, many of which derive from personal experience. If Jane favors boys of Fraternity XYZ, for example, then she may be attracted to Phil simply because he is a member. Similarly, if she thinks economics students are nerds, then she may refuse a first date with one regardless of whether he fits her personal definition of economics students. If your luggage is stolen while you are traveling in Italy, you may come to feel that Italians are dishonest. If you have seen several Swedish films starring beautiful actresses, perhaps you have come to believe that all Swedish women are beautiful.

In saner moments, we realize that although generalizations are necessary to the organization of any perceptions, generalizations based on very limited personal experience are often inaccurate and misleading. Jane may find that the next member of Fraternity XYZ she dates is a nerd. You may get to know members of a wonderful Italian family who practically take you into their home. The first Swedish girl you actually meet may be unattractive.

But how we perceive other human beings also depends on generalizations derived from our shared experiences as members of a given culture or society. In discussing the Müller-Lyer illusion, we observed that culture is a determinant of visual perception. From the standpoint of human communication it is even more significant that culture can be a determinant of person perception.

Culture   The influence of a culture on the person perception of its members is most directly seen in its stereotypes. A **stereotype** is *a generalization about a class of people, objects, or events that is widely held by a given culture.* We cannot say categorically that all stereotypes are false. According to one hypothesis, there is a kernel of truth in all of them. Thus, we can at least acknowledge that some are accurate enough to provide a very limited basis for making judgments about groups of people we hardly know. But when applied to a specific individual, most stereotypes are inappropriate and highly inaccurate—and many are false. Relying on stereotypes rather than on direct perceptions can result in embarrassing social situations and inappropriate responses.

There can be no doubt that race membership affects our perceptions of others. For example, an early study finds that we are better at recognizing pictures of members of our own race than of members of another (Malpass and Kravitz, 1969). And we often make false assumptions—and actually perceive inaccurately—when we judge on the basis of race. For example, consider the experience of many African Americans. In his book *Member of the Club*, Lawrence Otis Graham (1995), a prominent attorney, writes about a certain New York restaurant that he does not patronize:

> because its maitre d' is never at the second floor entry landing upon a guest's arrival, which has left me on three occasions to fend off incoming patrons who handed me their hats, jackets, and umbrellas for the coat check. And I almost always avoid restaurants with valet parking because of the times I've been handed keys by incoming white patrons who assume that I am there to park cars rather than waiting to have my own car delivered to the front door as I leave. (p. 91)

Even positive stereotypes can have damaging effects on intercultural communication. In this country, Asian Americans have generally been singled out as America's most "successful" minority, sometimes fostering resentment by others and subtle forms of discrimination. The mass media seem to have given special emphasis to the "success story" of Asian Americans. "Intelligent," "hard-working," "quiet," "soft-spoken," "well-mannered"—these were some of the all-too-predictable terms (Taylor and Stern, 1997). One Asian American reporter sees the problem this way:

> I think Asians are seen in one of three stereotypical ways: 1) victims or perpetrators of crime, 2) immigrant owners of Laundromats, restaurants or corner stores where the owners feud with the local black residents, or, 3) the braniac students, nerd doctors, engineers or hi-sci experts with pocket protectors. HELLO!!!??? (Cited in Mansfield-Richardson, 2000, p. 298)

In our culture, with its strong emphasis on youth, stereotyping by age is also quite common. Thus, many older people find that despite their professional experience, it is difficult to change jobs, and, in fact, some who have spent most of their working lives within a single company are passed over for promotions or even let go. Several books on finding jobs and changing careers advise those over fifty to consider eliminating their age, date of college graduation, and mention of early employment from their résumés. Stereotyping by age is especially apparent in the mass media.

Physical Attributes   Stereotypes also extend to physical attributes. Think of the longstanding American stereotype concerning the advantages of being blonde. A wide variety of rinses and dyes are available to all who wish to cover even the earliest signs of gray hair or simply to choose the hair color of the moment.

In discussing attractiveness, we saw that physical attributes have considerable influence on our first impressions. Each culture emphasizes certain facial cues. It might be the amount of makeup a woman wears or how she wears her hair or even whether she wears glasses. For example, in some cultures, people are regarded as more intelligent, reliable, and industrious when they wear glasses (Kleinke, 1986, p. 79). No doubt you have seen people who are aware of the power of this stereotype and exploit it to create an impression. It's the same impulse that makes the budding "professorial type" sport a pipe or the femme fatale take to smoking little cigars.

Do you know anyone your age with a baby face? People with baby faces have larger eyes in proportion to the rest of their face; their eyebrows are high and fine; their noses tend to be smaller and their lips are also more childlike. The baby-face stereotype, as it's called, also describes a person with fuller cheeks, a rounder face. The look of babies is disarming. We are drawn to them, and now current research shows that we are also drawn to baby-faced adults (Zebrowitz, 1997). What's more, the baby-face stereotype is universal across cultures.

Baby-faced people are perceived as warm, trusting, and trustworthy. People talk to and confide in them more readily—and research finds that "a babyface is likely to be helpful in the early stages of making friends and in the evocation of intimacy in established relationships" (p. 98). The downside of having a baby face is that you tend to be perceived as having less expertise and as being naive and submissive—and this can influence not only your social life but your professional life as well.

Stereotyping certainly exists in computer-mediated communication. For example, one study of text-based virtual communities found that often the participants formed images of other players on the basis of screen names. For example:

> *timberwolf* is a broad shouldered man who wears cotton flannel shirts with the sleeves rolled up and likes to spend a lot of time outdoors. He wears gold wire-frame glasses and his somewhat unruly brown hair is starting to go gray. He's from the Pacific Northwest so that explains the flannel shirt, pseudo-lumberjack outdoorsman part. The graying hair goes with his being a professor, as do the glasses, although the fact that they are gold wire-trim has more to do with his name and the fact that he doesn't capitalize it, a sort of understated elegance. (Jacobson, 1999, p. 8)

Some Effects of Stereotyping

In these examples of stereotyping, a person is considered to have attributes generally ascribed to the group of which he or she is a member. That person is not perceived as a unique human being but as a member of a certain category of human beings, whether it be actresses, Asian Americans, or college professors. In a sense, the person is judged in terms of context. Although some generalizations about categories are valuable to us in daily experience, generalizations about human beings—especially generalizations about how they think and how they are likely to behave—tend to distort our perceptions and to interfere with our ability to make accurate judgments. Unfortunately, personal generalizations or stereotypes cannot be eliminated simply by alerting the perceiver to their dangers.

One analysis of research about stereotypes finds at least four statements that seem warranted. First, stereotyping results from "cognitive biases stemming from illusory correlations between group membership and psychological attributes." Second, our stereotypes influence the way we process information—we remember less favorable information about out-groups and more favorable information about in-groups. Third, "stereotypes create expectancies (hypotheses) about others, and individuals try to confirm these expectancies." And last—and perhaps most significant from the standpoint of intercultural communication—our stereotypes operate as a constraint upon the communication behaviors of others, giving rise to behavior that then confirms our stereotypic expectations (Gudykunst and Ting-Toomey, 1988, pp. 136–137). (See Chapter 10 for a further discussion of stereotyping.)

Social Roles

Among the several social roles that influence how we perceive others and are ourselves perceived by others are work roles, student roles, sex-linked roles, and marital roles.

Work Roles

A classic example of how our work roles may alter perception is Zimbardo's so-called prison experiment (1971) in which students randomly assigned to be "guards" and others designated "prisoners" quickly came to see and respond to each other in stereotypical guard-prisoner fashion: The guards became cruel and unjust, the prisoners rebellious. Although planned to last for two weeks, the experiment was stopped after only six days. Students no longer thought like students, but like guards and prisoners. They truly lived their parts.

More recently, research on Hispanics and whites (Jones, 1991) supports the view that perceived differences in social status (as defined by work roles) influence ethnic stereotypes and that "occupational status . . . is often used to make rather confident judgments of personal attributes." According to this study, "occupational title appears to be a more central trait than ethnicity in determining American students' perceptions of people" (p. 475).

Student Roles

As for student roles, research on perceptions in the classroom finds that teachers perceive the model student as a communicator—"well-behaved, patient, controlled, and polite. He or she waits before speaking, listens intently and politely, sits quietly while others talk, and contributes clear and germane comments" (Trenholm and Rose, 1981, p. 24). Teachers describe the model student as one who willingly does all assignments, "never criticizes the teacher or gives way to frustration, and accepts and even welcomes criticism" (p. 24). According to these findings, compliance rather than inquiring behavior would be rewarded.

What a contrast with the way most students feel about unquestioning compliance. Years after she graduated from college, Sara McNeill could still recall the time she received an A for a paper she wrote for comparative lit while Nazik, the Iranian grad student sitting next to her, received only a B minus for hers. Sara knew she had only summarized and "played back" Dr. Kiernan's views. Nazik had taken a more controversial stance, and in class Dr. Kiernan had questioned her about it. A published author in her own country, Nazik was having difficulty slipping back into the role of student, and Dr. Kiernan was more interested in compliance than originality. He was not at all pleased by a student who challenged his analysis even when she was able to defend her point of view.

Another aspect of student–teacher roles is the perception of power in the classroom. Although teachers and students generally agree on power bases, some important differences exist. Both groups see most power as stemming from the teacher's ability to give rewards (e.g., high grades, approval), ability to make the student identify with the teacher, and perceived expertise. Again students, as you might expect, have a less positive view of the teacher's use of power (McCroskey and Richmond, 1983).

Sex-Linked Roles

That sex-linked roles also influence perceptions is confirmed by several research summaries. The consensus is that women are perceived as more supportive than men, laughing more often, intruding less on others, and being more deferential. Men, on the other hand, are considered more dominant and more achievement— and task—oriented. These descriptions reflect the more stereotypical views that women place a higher value on establishing and maintaining relationships while men tend to perceive the world more as a place to "win" or "achieve" (Rosenthal and DePaulo, 1979; LaFrance and Mayo, 1979; and Pearson et al., 1995).

Although in most studies males are perceived as more assertive in their communication style and females as more responsive, other research (Staley and Cohen, 1988; Bonaguro and Pearson, 1986) fails to find evidence of the latter. Staley and Cohen point out that little attention has been given to self-perceptions of male-female communication style, and their results indicate that, for the most part, males and females tend to see themselves similarly. They suggest that future investigations of sex differences in communicator style concentrate on actual behavior.

Others argue that a person whose self-concept is highly sex-typed may strive to maintain behavior consistent with various internalized standards for that role and to suppress behavior seen as inappropriate. They cite Bem's suggestion "that an androgynous self-concept might allow individuals to engage freely in both masculine and feminine behaviors and allow greater human potentiation" (Veenendall and Braito, 1987, p. 32).

Marital Roles

Perceptions of marital roles have undergone considerable change in the last decades, particularly with the great number of married women who have joined the workforce (Cherlin, 1998). A study attempting to predict marital and career success among dual-working couples (Hiller and Philliber, 1982) identifies four major marital types: These are based on how the husband and wife perceive themselves.

In a *traditional marriage relationship,* the husband sees himself as masculine and the wife sees herself as feminine. For example, although both work outside the home, the husband is perceived as bringing home the proverbial bacon whereas the wife has sole responsibility for all the housework. Housework is her province, and he won't help with any of it.

In a *reluctant wife marriage relationship,* the wife views herself as feminine and her husband sees himself as androgynous (having both masculine and feminine characteristics). If the wife in this relationship does not perceive herself as furnishing most of the emotional support, she may perceive her husband as "too feminine." And if her husband helps with the housework, sharing these tasks because she is so busy as a result of her successful career, she may feel guilty—both because she neglects "her duties" at home and because her professional skills seem "unfeminine."

On the other hand, in a *reluctant husband marriage relationship,* the husband sees himself as masculine and his wife sees herself as androgynous: He may feel threatened by her broad range of activities if he defines her role more narrowly. Suppose, for example, that she wants to split all the housework while he believes that if she hasn't the time for all the domestic concerns, she should spend less time at the office.

In the *androgynous marriage relationship,* the fourth type, both spouses see themselves as androgynous: Both engage in so-called masculine and feminine behaviors, making adaptation easier. He may even do most of the cooking, while she does most of the cleaning and laundry. Problems may still arise based on social expectations of appropriate or "proper" husband/wife roles.

It might be interesting to try classifying the marriages of those you know—relatives, friends, neighbors—and see whether you can discover any pattern related to age, work, and psychological makeup of the spouses involved. Or ask yourself which type of marriage you have or expect to have. (For a further discussion of marital roles, see Chapter 9.)

We've looked at several factors influencing our impressions of others. In addition to their physical attractiveness, expressiveness, and social roles, our own self-perceptions, our notions of personality, and the stereotypes we hold and our own generalizations also come into play. So we turn in the final section of this chapter to questions concerning the accuracy of these impressions.

SOME VARIABLES INVOLVED IN ACCURATE PERCEPTION

Granted the selective quality of human perception, we must ask what are the other variables that will affect the accuracy of our perceptions. Studies suggest that at least three generalizations can be made:

1. Some people are easier to judge than others—perhaps because they are more open about themselves.
2. Certain traits are easier to judge than others—e.g., it is much easier to identify people who are not shy than it is to pick out people who consider themselves shy (Zimbardo, 1990).
3. People are better at judging those who resemble themselves.

The Effect of Context   From what we know at present, it seems likely that the ability to judge other people may be quite specific to context. For example, students were asked to view a person bargaining, first in a very cooperative situation and later in a very competitive one. Group influence was so strong that when their perception of the bargainer did not correspond to the perceptions of other group members, subjects denied what they had seen with their own eyes. In fact, they came to believe the opposite of what they had seen. Majority or group opinion is just one instance in which context—the third element of perception—exerts its subtle influence.

Perceiver Self-Confidence   For a long time, psychologists have tried to establish whether some people are indeed better judges than others. Certainly, we all know people who feel their perceptions to be extremely accurate. But is there a relationship between self-confidence and accuracy? Does self-confidence about our ability to judge others make a difference in how we see them?

In terms of our communication model, we might say that a person who forms impressions of others solely on the basis of personal expectations avoids the task of person perception. Researchers have found no correlation between confidence in our perceptions of others and the accuracy of those perceptions.

Other Perceiver Traits   Despite the fact that accurate person perception varies from one situation to another, theorists generally agree that certain characteristics are associated with sound perceptions of others.

First, *intelligence* is a prime factor. Second, *the ability to draw inferences about people from their behavior* seems related to accurate perception. Third, people who score low on tests of authoritarianism tend to be better judges of others. They are *less rigid* in their *expectations,* judging more from what they know about the person and assuming less that he or she is like themselves. And fourth, those with *a high degree of objectivity* about themselves tend to have insight into the behavior of others. Openness and awareness of our own shortcomings seem to play a part in this process.

A recent survey of *empathic accuracy and inference,* how good we are at reading the thoughts and feelings of other people, finds that intelligence, cognitive complexity, positive adjustment, and interpersonal trust as well as social sensitivity—in combination—all play a part (Davis and Kraus, 1997, p. 163). And though women are generally regarded as being more intuitive, more empathic, Graham and Ickes say that although the stereotype of "women's intuition" might have a "proverbial kernel of truth, gender differences in empathic skills and dispositions appear to be small rather than large and specific rather than general in their scope." In general, though women "are indeed more accurate decoders than men of other people's nonverbal behavior . . . this relatively modest advantage applies primarily to the decoding of facial expressions that convey intended rather than unintended emotions" (1998, pp. 139–140).

How can this information be applied to improving our effectiveness as communicators? We certainly cannot improve our intelligence directly—and the ability to draw valid inferences about people from their behavior probably depends in part on intelligence. Nor can we simply tell ourselves to be less rigid or authoritarian. Research demonstrates that attitudes are rarely changed so easily.

One thing we can do is become conscious of, and less defensive about, our own limitations. And the more sensitive we become to cues outside ourselves, the more we listen instead of projecting our own feelings onto others, the more accurate we are likely to be in our evaluations of others.

IMPROVING PERCEPTION AND COMMUNICATION

Failures in communication frequently occur because people have inaccurate perceptions of each other. If a man is told that a woman he knows only casually is snobbish and standoffish, he is not very likely to ask her out. If you feel that a particular instructor is stubborn and somewhat hostile, you probably won't consider questioning her about your low grade on the last exam. But how do you know you are right? In many ways, your perceptions of others can determine not only the kind of communication that takes place but whether or not you attempt to communicate at all.

It would seem then an easy matter to facilitate communication by simply improving the accuracy of our perceptions. Yet the three elements of perception—perceiver, object, and context—are so interwoven that one cannot be analyzed apart from the others. One of the most important things the perceiver can do is take into account the need to make perceptual adjustments as any of these three components varies.

Among the primary elements in accurate person perception is an awareness that your own perceptions may be inaccurate. Improved perception and communication can occur only if you are willing to acknowledge that your perceptions are subjective. One of the authors remembers a conversation in which two people disagreed about their perceptions of a third. When one was asked whether she was sure of what she was saying, she replied, "Would I say it if it weren't true?" Her statement shows an obvious lack of awareness that human perceptions are subject to error. As long as she denied that possibility, there was little chance that an effective exchange of viewpoints could take place.

Another requirement is empathy. **Empathy** involves *experiencing the other's perception—that is, seeing and feeling things as the other does.* We've already seen in the research on behavior attribution how people tend to view their own behavior as response to a given situation and to interpret the same behavior in another person as an expression of stable traits or needs. For example, you lose your temper and explain you've had a hectic and frustrating day, but when one of your coworkers loses his temper, you say he has "a short fuse."

Ideally, we work toward developing the kind of sensitivity or responsiveness to others that actually extends perception. Many scholars believe empathy is the key to effective listening and therefore to communication. In Chapter 5, the role of empathy in listening and in resolving conflicts should become clear: Perceiving something the way the other person perceives it—taking the other's perspective—provides insights and paves the way for effective relationships.

It would be utopian to say that more accurate person perception always makes for more effective communication. Nevertheless, communication in both long-term and short-term relationships is often enhanced when the participants perceive each other accurately. The same principles apply to marital and dating relationships and to many less intense interpersonal encounters.

Consider the interview, for example. It relies heavily on accurate person perception even though the relationship is relatively short term. Here is a situation in which two or more people meet to exchange information—ordinarily about a subject that has been decided on beforehand—and to formulate impressions of one another. In a selection or job interview, it is each person's intention to size up the other's attributes. Person perception is one of the prime objectives. In an evaluative interview an employee's work is appraised by a supervisor, and guidelines for improved job performance are discussed. Several studies have shown that two of the most important objectives of evaluative interviews are that the employee perceive the supervisor as helpful and constructive rather than critical and that the supervisor and employee perceive effective job performance in a similar way.

We have tried to suggest that interpersonal sensitivity is important to both long- and short-term encounters. In the chapters that follow, we shall also see that although early impressions depend to a great extent on the perceiver's preconceptions and stereotypes and on the other person's physical appearance, as contact with a person continues, the content of his or her messages (both verbal and nonverbal) plays a greater role in modifying our perceptions of that person.

Summary

In this chapter, we looked at person perception as an active process in which communicators selectively perceive, organize, and interpret what they experience. We also showed how person perception affects intercultural communication. We began by considering the physiological and psychological filters that affect all our perceptions. After suggesting some parallels between object and person perception, we looked first at how we form our perceptions about ourselves. Thus, we examined some of the many variables that influence self-concept and particularly self-esteem, and looked at recent research findings about shyness. We then focused on how our impressions of other human beings are formed. We spoke of how we tend to view our own behaviors as opposed to those of others. We discussed trait centrality and associations of traits, primacy, and the effects of physical attractiveness and expressiveness. Personal generalizations and stereotypes and the influence of work, student, sex-linked, and marital roles were also discussed.

We saw that our impressions, while formed with relative ease, are not necessarily accurate. Some characteristics of perceivers were mentioned, but judging ability itself was seen as sometimes specific to context. In concluding, we discussed inaccurate perception as a source of communication failures and how improved perception enhances communication. Empathy was seen to be one of the crucial elements in this process.

Key Terms

Behavior attribution
CMC
Empathy
Expressiveness
Looking glass self

Perceptual filters
Primacy effect
Private theory of
    personality
Psychological sets

Selective attention
Self-concept
Self-esteem
Self-fulfilling prophecy
Stereotype

Go to the Online
Learning Center at
www.mhhe.com/
tubbsmoss for
glossary flashcards
and crossword
puzzles.

For further review, go
to the *Self-Quiz* on
the Online Learning
Center at
www.mhhe.com/
tubbsmoss.

Review Questions

1. Distinguish between a perceptual filter and a psychological set.

2. Discuss two ways in which person perception is different from object perception. What are the implications of these differences for communication?

3. Discuss the formation of self-concept and two important influences on self-esteem. Discuss the recent findings of self-esteem research.

4. Describe some of the new research findings about shyness, including shyness and Internet use.

5. What is the Pygmalion effect? Discuss some of the research on it.

6. Identify the single most significant implication of behavior attribution research for the study of person perception.

7. Explain the concept of central traits and its significance for person perception.

8. What is the primacy effect? How might it influence communication?

9. Give a brief summary of the major research findings on physical attractiveness and its influence on first impressions.

10. Explain how expressiveness affects person perception.

11. How do personal generalizations and stereotypes differ?

12. List four statements about stereotypes that are supported by recent research.

13. Describe the influence of work, sex-linked, student, and marital roles on how we perceive and are ourselves perceived by others.

14. What three generalizations can you make from the research studies cited here about how various traits of the perceived affect the accuracy of person perception?

15. Discuss four perceiver characteristics associated with accurate perception of others.

16. What are two ways in which person perception and communication effectiveness can be improved?

17. Explain the concept of empathy and its significance for accurate person perception.

Exercises

1. Select one of the case problems listed in the appendix. The appendix can be found at *www.mhhe.com/tubbsmoss*. Ask five people to read the same case problem and each to write a short paper supporting a solution to the problem. Examine the solutions offered in terms of differences and similarities in person perception. Explain how the following concepts relate to the similarities and differences:

    a. Psychological set

    b. Psychological filter

    c. Primacy effect

    d. Stereotype perceptions

2. Write a description of yourself in which you use ten adjectives. Then ask a person in your class to describe you in the same way, and compare the results. You might try this again with a close friend.

3. Go to *www.shyness.com* and answer the thirty-five questions on the Henderson/Zimbardo Shyness Questionnaire. Then to get your ShyQ or rating (Not Shy to Very Shy), go to the results section. Share these results with two friends. Do you think the rating is accurate? Do your friends? You can also participate in research on computer-mediated communication by filling out the Social Interaction and Technology Use Questionnaire at the same website.

4. Write down some of the perceptions you have of your classmates. Then refer to your earlier comments in the personal log on the computer that you began in Chapter 1, exercise 1. Have you changed or confirmed some of your original impressions?

5. Reread your descriptions (in exercise 4) of people who really impressed you at first. Write a list of words describing each person. Then try to identify the specific verbal and nonverbal behaviors that led you to draw up each list. Now that you know each of these people better, what additional experiences have shaped your perception of each of them?

6. Write a paragraph describing someone you think is an effective communicator. List all attributes that seem to contribute to this effectiveness. Now think of a poor communicator. What characteristics seem to cause the ineffectiveness?

7. What characteristics do you possess that affect how you perceive these two people?

8. Have the class split up into groups of five. Your instructor will give you copies of the "Preliminary Scale of Interpersonal Perceptions." Fill out these forms, giving your perceptions of each of the other members in your group. Do not put your own name on the forms. When everyone has filled out all the forms, exchange them so that each person has a

rating from every other group member. Then look at the ratings you received from the rest of the group. You might want to discuss these with others in the group to gain additional feedback. Interview a person who does a lot of interviewing. Discuss communication and person perception with that person. Have the interviewer elaborate on how he or she perceives interviewees and selects cues in assessing them.

Suggested Readings

Cole, Jonathan. *About Face.* Bradford Books, 1999.

A study of the human face, its expressiveness, and what happens to people who lose their capacity to make facial expressions. The author presents research on the importance of the face in the development of communication and emotion.

Cheek, Jonathan, and Bronwen Cheek. *Conquering Shyness.* New York: Dell, 1990.

The authors discuss shyness and outline a treatment program for overcoming shyness and building self-esteem.

Crozier, W. Ray (ed.). *Shyness: Development, Consolidation and Change.* New York: Routledge, 2000.

An important collection of work on the study of shyness. For the advanced student.

Kenny, David. *Interpersonal Perception.* New York: Guilford, 1994.

A social relations approach to interpersonal perception.

Ickes, William, ed. *Empathic Accuracy.* New York and London: Guilford, 1997.

An excellent collection of essays on many aspects of empathic accuracy. See, especially, Chapter 5 on the limits of women's intuition and Chapter 6 on the relationship between personality and empathic accuracy.

Zebrowitz, Leslie A. *Reading Faces: Window to the Soul?* Boulder, CO: Westview Press, 1997.

A fascinating discussion of research and theory about self-fulfilling prophecies as well as responses to baby-faced people and physical attractiveness in general.

Zimbardo, Philip G. *Shyness: What It Is, What to Do about It.* Reading, MA: Addison-Wesley, 1990.

A classic on the nature of shyness.

The Verbal Message

Chapter Objectives

After reading this chapter, you should be able to:

1. Explain what is intended by the statement "The word is not the thing," and distinguish between denotation and connotation.
2. Differentiate between private and shared meanings, and explain the concepts of overlapping codes and codeswitching.
3. Discuss two theories about how message encoding skills develop.
4. Summarize the Sapir-Whorf hypothesis, and describe two ways in which language and thought are related.
5. Specify five problem areas in our use of language, and give an example of each.
6. Explain how one's cultural frame of reference influences communication, and give examples from two different cultures.
7. Discuss the effects of sexist language on communication, how male and female language usage differs, and several language forms perceived by others as powerful.
8. Explain the concept of metacommunication, and give an example.

In the fall of 2001, eight U.S. senators and movie stars along with Rabbi Chaim Feld, head of Aish Hatorah, an international Orthodox Jewish educational organization, launched a media campaign to stop the harmful use of words in our society. Their new organization is called Words Can Heal (see *www.wordscanheal.org*). Some of the stars included Tom Cruise, Nicole Kidman, Whoopi Goldberg, and Bette Midler. This is one of the most public pronouncements demonstrating people's awareness of the positive and negative power of words (Reuters, 2001, p. 5A).

The word "conversation" is the same in English and French, but as Raymonde Carroll explains, "It is far from signifying the same thing in the two cultures." Words per se cannot be said to "contain" meaning. As we will see, even for people who share a common language, words often generate very different associations (Carroll, 1988, p. 23).

As we examine verbal messages in this chapter, we will take up four major concerns. The first is the relationship between words and meaning. Thus, we will be talking about the symbolic nature of language, the descriptive and associative aspects of words (denotation and connotation), as well as private and shared meanings.

A second section takes up the complex process of formulating verbal messages and how we all learn to do this. As we examine the next issue, how language and thought are related, you will learn about a highly influential theory on the subject, the Sapir-Whorf hypothesis, and then look at several ways in which language use—abstraction, for example—affects your thinking.

In the concluding section, you will also learn about the influence of language usage on feelings and behavior. You will be looking at sexist language, gender differences in the use of language, and the linguistic forms considered more powerful or effective.

Let's turn first to a consideration of the nature of language.

WORDS AND MEANING

We saw in Chapter 1 that the communication process involves sending messages from one person's nervous system to another's with the intention of creating a meaning similar to the one in the sender's mind. The verbal message does this through words, the basic elements of language, and words, of course, are verbal symbols.

Symbols and Referents

In Chapter 1, we defined a **symbol** as *something used for or regarded as representing something else.* Thus, the image of a lion can serve as a symbol of courage, a red-and-white striped pole as a symbol of a barber shop. In English, the word "sun" is the verbal symbol used to designate the star that is the central body of our solar system; the French use another symbol, "soleil"; and the Germans a third, "Sonne." All three symbols represent the same star.

Consider the term "disk." "Disk" is the name given to a flexible, round magnetic recording medium or storage device. The term is arbitrary. It was assigned to the recording device so that we could communicate about it without pointing each time we referred to it. "Disk" might have been called "soft record" or "blank" or even "urg." So initially, no real association exists between a word we agree to call something and its **referent,** *the object for which it stands.* Clearly, the word is not the thing. A word is merely a verbal symbol of the object it represents. Such words as "teletext," "modem," "digital information system," and "e-mail" are but a few of those that have entered our language as a result of the new communication technologies. Another recent example is the Amway company, which sometimes uses high-pressure tactics to sell products through friendship networks. Amway launched its e-commerce business with a new name Quixtar in October of 2000. The corporate leaders wanted to differentiate its new line of business from the traditional view of the company named Amway. It also changed the Amway name to Alticor for the same reason. Amway had just developed a negative brand image (Bott, 2000, p. F1). See also, *www.quixtar.com.*

Once we agree on a system of verbal symbols, we can use language to communicate. Of course, if all the words we used referred only to objects, our communication problems would be eased considerably. We could establish what referents we were speaking about with somewhat less difficulty. But words also refer to events, properties of things, actions, relationships, concepts, and so on. Take the words "white lie." Suppose one of your friends tells you something that is not true and you find out and confront her with your knowledge. Although she explains that it was just a "white lie," you may consider her action a form of "deception"—it's even possible that an argument will ensue. And if you can't reach agreement on relatively simple terms, what about terms that represent higher levels of abstraction? What are the referents of such terms as "ethics," "freedom," and "responsibility"?

The relationship between meaning and reference becomes especially clear when we encounter words in a foreign language. If we see **МИР**, the Russian word for "peace" and "world," for the first time, we have no way of determining what concepts that word represents simply by looking at the word itself. Even with new words in our own language, we have to learn what concepts they represent. Notice how we carefully avoided saying, "what the words mean." Meanings are not inherent in words. Words in and of themselves are meaningful only after we have associated them with some referents. It is human beings who assign meanings to words.

Denotation and Connotation

In discussing meaning, some students of language make the traditional distinction between "denotation" and "connotation." We have said that words are meaningful only after we have associated them with some referents. When we speak of **denotation,** we refer to *the primary associations a word has for most members of a given linguistic community.* When we speak of **connotation,** we refer to *other,*

secondary associations a word has for one or more members of that community.
Sometimes the connotations a word has are the same for nearly everyone; sometimes they relate solely to one individual's experience or, more often, to the experience of a particular subgroup.

The connotations of words are often the occasion for misunderstanding. For
example, when you see the term "flight attendant" what do you picture? Would
it be a 78-year-old woman? Probably not. However, Norma Webb is Delta Airlines's oldest flight attendant, with 52 years of flying experience beginning in
1946 (Frankel and Pierce, 1998, pp. 63–64).

Did you know that after ten years of falling sales, the prune industry decided to officially change the name of that fruit to "dried plums"? The California
Prune Board spent over $10 million in 2001 to market its new brand image. The
term "dried plums" tested much more positively by 90 percent of those surveyed.
Similarly, Kiwi fruit used to be known as Chinese gooseberries, but the name was
changed for better marketing and sales (Condor, 2001, p. 5H).

Did you also know that SPAM means a spiced lunch meat product made of
pork shoulders and ham which is sold by Hormel Foods Corporation? To many
young people spam means junk (unwanted) e-mail. Hormel Foods went to court
to ensure that when you use the word in upper case letters SPAM it refers to their
product and when you use spam in lowercase letters it refers to junk e-mail. According to one source, "The slang meaning of 'spam' is said to have been inspired
by a skit by British comedy troupe Monty Python in which a group of Vikings
mutter 'spam, spam, spam,' with an ever increasing volume, drowning out normal
conversation" (Reuters, 2001, p. B13). (See also, *www.spam.com/ci/ci_in.htm.*)

In the 2000 Census, over 22 million people living in the United States indicated that they were of "Spanish/Hispanic Origin"—the term used by the Census
Bureau—yet many reject "Hispanic." Some say "Hispanic" is a term associated
with colonization; others that it carries the connotation of "social striving, a desire to be accepted at any cost, even by using an 'English' word." Many younger
people prefer "Latino," a word they feel connotes respect. And there seems to be
a growing preference to reject those labels, and their stereotypes, entirely: According to a recent nationwide survey, "Most Hispanics/Latinos prefer to identify
themselves as Puerto Rican, Colombian, Dominican, or just plain American."
(We should add that in textbooks such as this, the decision to use one term, "Hispanics," for example, is based on the need to describe research findings in the
words used by the researchers cited.)

On a much lighter note, Scotti and Young (1997) have compiled an entire
book of words with their connotations in the Los Angeles area, which they call
"L.A. Freshspeak." Some examples are:

To clock: To check something out: "that biddy's been clocking me all night."

Himbo: a male bimbo.

Nimrod: a geek.

Soap on a rope: a dull or depressed person.

Spliced: married.

Squid: a nerd.

Starter marriage: one's first, which is not expected to last.

Tard: stupid or insensitive person (retarded). Also, tardo, tardie, and tard off (obnoxious).

Tenderoni: a sweet young thing, a girlfriend.

Wigger: a person prone to outbursts of temper (who wigs out).

Winnie Bago: an obese person, usually male.

Zootie: a streetwise girl, a little rough around the edges. (pp. 16–33)

Negative-Positive Connotation

Because words can elicit such powerful emotional reactions, they are often said to have negative or positive connotations for people. Today, many people prefer to be called "senior citizens" rather than "elderly." And though parents may take equal pleasure in hearing their children referred to as "brilliant" or "gifted," those with "retarded" children are sensitive to the many negative connotations of the word.

Another example is writer/actress Eve Ensler's play entitled *The Vagina Monologues*. She said the title evolved out of a sense of shame. "No matter how many times you say it, it never sounds like a word you want to say, and there's no reason to feel that way," says the New York–based Ensler. The idea for the play, which is against violence toward women, grew out of interviews with over 200 women, young, married, single, college professors, actors, corporate professionals, and even sex counselors. All expressed strong aversion to just the word itself (Potter, 2001, p. F1).

In another example, a few years ago Reebok named a women's running shoe "Incubus" without knowing that the term "incubus" means a mythical demon who rapes sleeping women. Reebok later said that it was "horrified" about the mistake and immediately discontinued the use of the offensive name (*Detroit Free Press,* February 20, 1997, p. E1).

In research on word connotations, subjects were exposed to various words on a tachistoscope, and their galvanic skin responses were measured. Although there were nonsignificant differences between responses to "good" words (e.g., "beauty," "love," "kiss," and "friend") and "aversive" words (e.g., "cancer," "hate," "liar," and "death"), some words caused significant reactions in both men and women. These were called "personal" words and included the subject's first name, last name, father's first name, mother's first name, major in school, year in school, and school name. Subjects were more physiologically aroused by the personal words than by either the good or the aversive words (Crane et al., 1970). (For a discussion entitled "What Makes Bad Language Bad?" see Davis, 1989.)

The Semantic Differential

Some of the most influential research on the measurement of meaning has been conducted by Osgood and his associates (1957), who developed an instrument called the **Semantic Differential.** With the Semantic Differential, a researcher *can test a person's reactions to any concept or term*—sex, hard rock, mother, political correctness, apartheid, ego, cigarettes, Madonna, capital punishment—and then compare them with those of other people.

The test itself is a seven-interval scale with limits defined by sets of bipolar adjectives. "The words used to anchor the scales," explains Griffin (1991), "are concerned with feelings (connotation) rather than a description (denotation)" (p. 32). Figure 3.1, for example, is a Semantic Differential for the word "commitment." The subject rates the concept by checking the interval between each pair of adjectives that best describes it. The researcher then draws a line connecting each point made by the subject, thus creating a profile of the subject's concept of commitment.

Statistical analysis of the work of Osgood and his associates suggests that our judgments have three major dimensions: evaluation, potency, and activity. Thus, we say that commitment is good or bad and cruel or kind (evaluation), that it is powerful or weak and hot or cold (potency), and fast or slow and active or passive (activity).

Culture and Connotation

The subjects of Osgood's early research were Americans, but he was intrigued by the possibility of cross-cultural studies and went on to explore the dimensions of affective meaning in 26 different language communities (Osgood, 1974a; 1974b). According to Osgood, the major dimensions of affective meaning in all these cultures were the same: evaluation, potency, and activity.

From his cross-cultural research, Osgood has compiled the *Atlas of Affective Meanings.* The 620 concepts in this atlas run the gamut from "accepting things as they are," "accident," "marriage," and "masculinity," to "master," "yesterday," "youth," and "zero." Although Osgood found certain definite cultural variations, many concepts were evaluated similarly by members of a great many different cultures. One such concept was "the days of the week." Monday was generally evaluated as the worst day in the week; things tended to improve after that, gathering momentum on Friday and reaching a peak on Sunday, the best day. For Iranians, on the other hand, the worst day was Saturday (comparable to our Monday), and Friday (the Moslem holy day) was the best (Osgood, 1974b, p. 83).

The great appeal of the Semantic Differential is its flexibility. The procedure is so general that it can be precisely tailored to the needs and interests of the experimenter, who can test the emotional valence of any concept at all.

Griffin (1991) offers this assessment of Osgood's work:

Of course, many anthropologists doubt the validity of Osgood's conclusion that evaluation, potency, and activity are universal dimensions of affect. Anyone who

Figure 3.1

Commitment

Sharp	_____ : _____ : _____ : _____ : _____ : _____ : _____	Dull
Courageous	_____ : _____ : _____ : _____ : _____ : _____ : _____	Cowardly
Dirty	_____ : _____ : _____ : _____ : _____ : _____ : _____	Clean
Hot	_____ : _____ : _____ : _____ : _____ : _____ : _____	Cold
Good	_____ : _____ : _____ : _____ : _____ : _____ : _____	Bad
Fair	_____ : _____ : _____ : _____ : _____ : _____ : _____	Unfair
Powerful	_____ : _____ : _____ : _____ : _____ : _____ : _____	Weak
Deceitful	_____ : _____ : _____ : _____ : _____ : _____ : _____	Honest
Fast	_____ : _____ : _____ : _____ : _____ : _____ : _____	Slow
Cruel	_____ : _____ : _____ : _____ : _____ : _____ : _____	Kind
Active	_____ : _____ : _____ : _____ : _____ : _____ : _____	Passive

claims they've punched a hole in the language barrier is bound to draw fire. But a decade of rigorous cross-cultural testing with the semantic differential suggests that Osgood has made a quantum leap in understanding the meaning of meaning. (p. 36)

Private and Shared Meanings

In psychology and semantics, much research is based on the distinction between denotation and connotation. The Semantic Differential, for example, is said to measure "connotative meaning." But when we examine it closely, the distinction between denotation and connotation seems to break down. All people who speak English are members of the same linguistic community; yet within that community certain groups exist for whom even the primary associations, or denotations, of a given word are different.

Take the case of the Americans and the British. In England you take a "lift," not an "elevator"; if you ask for the "second floor," you get the "third." You take the "underground," not the "subway." You "queue up"; you don't "stand in line." You go to a "chemist's," not a "pharmacy." The list seems virtually endless.

Private Meaning

We can all use language idiosyncratically, assigning meanings to words without agreement and, in effect, creating our own private language. We can decide, for example, to call trees "reds" or "cows" or "haves." Schizophrenic speech is often private in this way, but schizophrenics are unaware that they sometimes use language in a way that is not shared by others: They use the words they have re-created and expect to be understood. When one young patient was admitted to a hospital, she continually referred to her father, a lawyer by profession, as "the chauffeur." Everyone with whom she spoke found this reference bizarre. Only in treatment was it learned that when she called her father a "chauffeur," she meant that he was completely under her mother's domination.

Shared Meaning

Presumably, if we assign private meanings to words, we are aware that we can use them to communicate with someone only if we let that person know what the referents of these words are. **Shared meaning** requires *some correspondence between the message as perceived by the sender and the receiver.* Two friends, a husband and wife, an entire family, or a group of physicists may decide to use language in a way that makes little sense to others. Among themselves, however, they can communicate with no difficulty.

The same phenomenon occurs among members of many other kinds of groups. Actors understand each other when they talk about scenes being "blocked." Physical therapists refer in their work to "trigger points" and "jelling pain." There is an extensive vocabulary that describes the various moves possible on a skateboard. Skateboard enthusiasts talk about "ollies," "bonelesses," "720s," "thread the needles," and "slob airs." For the subgroup that uses this language, the meaning of "bonelesses" and "thread the needles" is always clear.

One writer described the insider language of those who approve screenplays for major motion pictures such as producers, directors, and lead actors. He wrote that when people use the following terms they really mean something else: "Wonderful means change it. Fantastic means change it. Terrific means change it. Thank you means you're fired" (Applebome, 1998, p. E1).

Group members have no difficulty understanding one another when they use language in this way because they share a code. Communication difficulties emerge only when they expect meaning to be shared by those outside the group. This is a recurring expectation, especially in a country such as the United States, where so many different ethnic groups coexist.

Overlapping Codes and Codeswitching

In intercultural communication, the sender and the receiver often have **overlapping codes,** "*codes which provide an area of commonality but which also contain areas of unshared codification*" (Smith, in Samovar and Porter, 1972, p. 291, emphasis added). Even if the code they use at home is very different, members of minority groups are usually compelled to learn and make some use of the language of the majority because in education, business, and politics this language dominates.

Restricted codes of communication seem to be common among intimate dyads. A study of young lovers (Bell et al., 1987) found the number of personal idioms they used—that is, "words, phrases, or nonverbal signs they had created that had meaning unique to their relationship" (p. 47)—to be highly correlated with love, commitment, and closeness. This proved to be true for both premarital and marital relationships. The couples studied had private idioms, which they used only when they were alone, and public idioms, which they could use when others were present: The private idioms were usually sexual references or euphemisms and sexual invitations (e.g., "Let's go home and watch TV"), whereas the public idioms were often nicknames, confrontations, teasing insults, and requests.

Shifts in codes occur in many different communication contexts. An analysis of such American television interviewers as Mike Wallace, Phil Donahue, and Tom Snyder (Scotton, 1988) argues that a pattern of frequent codeswitching within a single conversation can be used by a speaker for the purpose of negotiating power. **Codeswitching** is referred to here as *shifting to different styles* (casual, quasi-literary, and so on) *and introducing shifts in vocabulary or syntax.* There are many contexts in which codeswitching establishes or reinforces intimacy. Novelist Amy Tan (1991), author of *The Joy Luck Club,* writes of speaking to an audience about her life and work when suddenly her talk sounded "wrong." Her language was formal and literary, but her mother, who was born in China, was in the audience and had never heard her speaking this formally. Tan goes on to describe how later, when taking a walk with her mother, she once more became aware of the English she was using:

> We were talking about the price of new and used furniture and I heard myself saying this: "Not waste money that way." My husband was with us as well, and he didn't notice any switch in my English. And then I realized why. It's because over the twenty years we've been together I've often used the same kind of English with him, and sometimes he even uses it with me. It has become our language of intimacy, a different sort of English that relates to family talk, the language I grew up with. (p. 197)

The several "Englishes" used by Tan will also be familiar to children of bilingual families.

MESSAGE ENCODING: A CHILD'S USE OF LANGUAGE

"You're lying," "I don't think you are telling the truth," "Fibber," "I don't believe you," "You liar"—these are alternate ways of formulating a single message, and there are many others. We use "Fibber" in one context, "You're lying" in another, and "I don't believe you" in a third, and we seem to make these distinctions without effort. Occasionally we wonder how to broach a delicate subject, but most of the time we speak without deliberation. Yet encoding a message is a complex process, however straightforward the message may be. Samovar and Porter (1991) define **encoding** as *"an internal activity in which verbal and nonverbal behaviors are selected and arranged according to the rules of grammar and syntax applicable to the language being used to create a message"* (emphasis added). In short, when we encode a message, we must have some awareness of the receiver if we want to be understood. The other half of the process is **decoding**—that is, *"the [receiver's] internal processing of a message and the attribution of meaning to the source's behaviors that represent the source's internal state of being."*

A look at how children use language gives us a better understanding of what takes place in the encoding process. Children astonish adults with their verbal facility. The three-year-old can formulate sentences, repeat all sorts of long words and colloquial expressions, and use several tenses correctly. Some three-year-olds have a vocabulary of nearly 1,000 words. The five-year-old speaks in correct, finished sentences and even uses complex sentences with hypothetical and conditional clauses. At this age the structure and form of language are essentially complete. But what about the encoding abilities of the child?

3.1 | **ISSUES IN COMMUNICATION**   *A Word about Semantics*

When do words make a difference? When you give someone your "word," what does that imply? Have you ever seen communication difficulties arise over the use and assumed meaning ascribed to certain words?

Hillary Rodham Clinton called her involvement in an Arkansas real estate deal "minimal." *Newsweek* states that it was about an hour a week for 15 months. What word would you use to describe that amount of work?

When Chevrolet introduced the Nova into Spanish-speaking countries, it had disappointing sales. *No va* means "it does not go" in Spanish. How could this be avoided?

When AT&T lays off 40,000 employees, it is called "downsizing" or "restructuring." What do you think it would be called if 40,000 people were permanently put out of work by an act of nature?

Some authors (Haney, 1992; Tubbs, 2001) have referred to different types of words as "purr" words versus "snarl" words. Imagine a work situation in which someone has just submitted a report and you want to give the person some feedback that you think it has some good aspects, but it could be improved. Try creating two scenarios in which you give the feedback using "snarl" words and another using "purr" words.

Egocentric Speech

To study the functions of language in children, the Swiss psychologist Jean Piaget (1962) made exhaustive observations and analyses of the way children speak both when they are alone and when they are in the company of other children. He also devised a series of experiments to determine how objective children try to be in communicating information.

A typical Piaget experiment follows this pattern. A child is shown a diagram of a water tap—sometimes Piaget uses a diagram of a bicycle—and given a precise explanation of how it works. Once it has been established that the child understands the experimenter's explanation, he or she is asked to repeat it (with the aid of the diagram) to another child. Piaget found that though a child fully understood an explanation, he or she was not necessarily successful in communicating it to another child.

Why should this be? It is not that the child lacks the necessary vocabulary. Nor is he or she by any means inarticulate. Piaget's work led him to the conclusion that in the child under age seven or eight, language has two distinct functions and that two kinds of speech exist: egocentric and socialized speech.

As Piaget describes patterns of **egocentric speech** in the child, he gives us a perfect example of a poor encoder, someone whose *speech does not adapt information to the receiver:*

> Although he talks almost incessantly to his neighbours, he rarely places himself at their point of view. He speaks to them for the most part as if he were thinking aloud. He speaks, therefore, in a language which . . . above all is always making assertions, even in argument, instead of justifying them . . . The child hardly ever even asks himself whether he has been understood. For him, that goes without saying, for he does not think about others when he talks. (1962)

Piaget believes that until a child is seven or eight, egocentric language constitutes almost half of his or her spontaneous speech, and his book, *The Language and Thought of the Child,* is full of amusing "conversations" between children in which virtually no communication takes place. For instance:

L.: "Thunder rolls."

P.: "No, it doesn't roll."

L.: "It's water."

P.: "No, it doesn't roll."

L.: "What is thunder?"

P.: "Thunder is . . ." (He doesn't go on.) (1962)

In contrast to egocentric speech, **socialized speech** involves *adapting information to the receiver and in some sense adopting his or her point of view;* it involves *social rather than nonsocial encoding.* Piaget goes beyond his findings about language to argue that the adult "thinks socially, even when he is alone, and . . . the child under 7 thinks egocentrically, even in the society of others" (1962).

One team of researchers went on to a further examination of this discrepancy between the communication skills of children and adults. Their strategy was to create a communication problem in the form of a game called "Stack the Blocks." Pairs of children, separated by an opaque screen so that they could not see each other, were given sets of blocks with designs that had **low codability**—that is, they were *difficult to describe.* Describing the design of the block so that the listener could identify it and stack his or her blocks in the same order was the communication problem.

The children's descriptions showed little social encoding. For example, one block was described by different children as "somebody running," "eagle," "throwing sticks," "strip-stripe," and "wire." In the role of speaker, some kindergartners and first-graders made comments such as "It goes like this," using one finger to trace the design in the air—which of course the listener could not see because he or she was behind a screen (Krauss, in Walcher, 1971). In general, children tended to use private rather than socially shared images; as a result their messages were often idiosyncratic.

Variations of the Stack the Blocks experiment had been conducted with children of all grade levels as well as with adults. Although nursery school children seem totally unable to complete this communication task, effectiveness in communication clearly increases with age (as measured by grade level).

According to Piaget's view, then, the speech of children, even at age seven, is of necessity egocentric. Thus, they are unable to encode messages effectively for the benefit of others. Their competence in communicating is linked with physical and intellectual development.

Sociocentric Speech

In recent years, most theorists and researchers have come to look upon communication as developing through interaction—that is, as a social phenomenon. Elliott (1984) argues, based on a broad summary of research, that the child is not egocentric but rather **sociocentric**—that is, *centered on social interaction*—from birth. The development of competence in communication is seen as a three-part process: The initial interaction between infant and mother is described as *primordial sharing;* this leads to *proto-conversation,* which ultimately leads to *conversation.*

Primordial sharing refers to *the mother's exchanges with the infant*—through grimaces, glances, vocalizations, and so on—*and, soon after, the infant's responses.* This is a "you and me" stage of communication: Meaning and context are not differentiated; "you" and "me" are, in effect, both the context and the meaning. Exchanges between mother and infant convey mutual attention and recognition. Infant and mother appear to engage in a coordinated interaction:

mutual attention, responsiveness, turn taking, and synchrony of signals. If either mother or infant is unresponsive, there is no interaction, no context, no meaning.

Once mother and infant direct attention to some object outside their pair, **proto-conversations** begin. Infants as young as four weeks attend to objects in their environment. In the next few months, the mutual regard of other objects is supplemented by other actions—for example, alternate gazes to object and other, infant babbling, and development of interpretable gestures such as pointing. These proto-conversations can be characterized by "you, me, and it." The extension to objects permits a range of meanings and so, for the first time, meaning may be ambiguous (a child points and the mother interprets the possible object, the reasons for pointing, and so on). By the age of three or four, the child's proto-conversation has become pretty successful for taking communicative action. Proto-conversation is limited, however, by what can be pointed to or indicated.

Conversation, the third phase, begins when *the context within which interactive meanings are generated includes references to entities and situations that are not present;* these may be imaginary or even unknown. Although meaning is distinguished from context in proto-conversation, the context in conversation is far larger; now meaning and action may be generated within the interaction itself.

The child's development of conversational abilities has been traced by Haslett, who looks at four aspects of the child's "increasing understanding of how conversational exchanges take place" (1984, p. 107). Four areas of competence are developed out of social interaction. First comes the child's understanding of the value of communication. According to Haslett, human beings seem to have an innate grasp of interpersonal interaction; this sense that through communication we establish relationships may correspond to Elliott's notion of being sociocentric. Thus, children are motivated, perhaps innately, to communicate with others. The infant explores communication by interacting with an adult caretaker—in Western cultures, usually the mother.

The second stage is reached when the infant's behavior becomes less idiosyncratic and more conventional—that is, it takes on more of the characteristics of generally agreed-upon communication signals. Now infants communicate intentionally: They check adults for feedback, alter their signals when adult behavior changes, and shorten and ritualize signals so that they become more conventional. The effort, then, is to enter a world of shared meanings. Over time the child progresses from intent-to-act (usually on physical objects) to intent-to-convey (the expression of content). During the course of interaction, the infant's use of words becomes more accountable through the mother's responses—that is, the mother and child negotiate meaning.

The third stage of the child's development concerns understanding the nature of conversation. While many of the infant's first communications were monologues, dialogues (conversations) represent a *joint negotiation of meaning between two parties.* Before understanding the nature of conversation, the child must recognize four fundamentals:

1. Conversations have signals that indicate beginnings and endings.
2. Conversations require both speaking and listening.
3. Roles reverse during conversation; you listen sometimes and speak at other times.
4. Participants reverse roles by taking turns. (Haslett, 1984, p. 113)

Thus, children learn to appreciate the requirements of human dialogue.

A final step in acquiring conversational competence is learning to develop a conversational style. The particular style a child will adopt depends on his or her interaction with the mother. Mothers *interpret* what their children say and thus help them express intentions in conventional ways. They *model* and thus socialize children into culturally acceptable ways of communicating. They also *extend* what their children say by responding in challenging ways. They *provide opportunities for conversation,* thus helping children gain strategies for the topics and opportunities for interaction given them. And finally, mothers *demonstrate positive attitudes toward communication.* Thus, the caretaker has a critical role in developing the child's conversational abilities (Haslett, 1984, p. 120).

In contrast to Piaget's view, the sociocentric view is that message-encoding skills begin to develop when we are very young children and these skills evolve out of our exchanges with other human beings. So a child learns early on and is learning all the time, given favorable conditions, to participate in that world of shared meanings first introduced by the mother or some other adult caretaker.

As adults, we differ in our sensitivity to conversation. Some of us are particularly savvy, others take conversations pretty much at face value. Qualities of both attention and interpretation would seem to be involved. For example, not everyone you speak with can sense when you are trying to end the conversation. Recently, a study (Kellerman et al., 1991) examined strategies people use to retreat when the decision to end conversation is not mutual. The researchers identified excuses, hints ("Well, . . . take care," "I wish I had more time to talk"), and departure announcements ("See you later," "I have to go now") as the most appropriate behaviors; excuses, departure announcements, and rejection as most efficient. Being unresponsive and changing the topic were least efficient. It seems that a person's ability to make it *appear* that the end of a conversation was arrived at mutually is particularly effective and involves skillful message encoding.

Another study of the components of conversational sensitivity finds that people high in sensitivity have a great capacity to remember what is being said, are perceptive in identifying deeper and sometimes multiple meanings, enjoy listening to social exchanges (even if they are not speaking), understand various kinds of power relationships in play, can sense patterns of affinity between people, are at ease with conversational word play, and can come up with extremely effective alternatives during conversation (Daly et al., 1987, p. 171). The researchers also report a correlation between high conversational sensitivity and high ratings for empathy, assertiveness, self-monitoring, and self-esteem.

LANGUAGE AND THOUGHT

In discussing message encoding, we've seen that language and thought are often said to be interrelated. But the nature of their relationship is far from clear. Is language a precondition of human thought? Is thinking simply inner speech? There are no easy answers. Students of communication have been particularly concerned with the question: Does language shape our ideas, or is it merely an instrument of thought?

The Sapir-Whorf Hypothesis

One version of the view that our thought is shaped by the language we speak is the **Sapir-Whorf hypothesis** that *the world is perceived differently by members of communities and that this perception is transmitted and sustained by language.* Benjamin Lee Whorf (1956), whose work was shaped by that of the great linguist Edwin Sapir, regards language as the primary vehicle of culture. In short, the language we speak influences our experience of the world, while the evolution of language also reflects changes in the predominant modes of expression.

Whorf supports this theory with findings from studies of Native American languages. In English, he points out, we tend to classify words as nouns or verbs; in Hopi the words tend to be classified by duration. For example, in Hopi "lightning," "flame," "wave," and "spark" are verbs, not nouns; they are classified as events of brief duration. In Nootka, which is spoken by the inhabitants of Vancouver Island, categories such as things and events do not exist; thus it is said that "A house occurs" or "It houses."

In an even more significant example, Stoltz (1997) cites brain research that shows that the language we use can shape our perception of success, and even our ability to be successful. Those individuals who tell themselves that their shortcomings are long lasting tend to have more failures than those who see setbacks as temporary. Similarly, those who see setbacks as a result of their lack of abilities tend to have more failures than those who see their failures as a result of not having given their best effort. This research has major implications for helping people improve their career and life successes.

Relabeling skills are what Losoncy (1997) calls the ability to use language in more constructive ways. For example, one can relabel setbacks as "annoyances," catastrophes as "hindrances," failures as "growth experiences," or rejections as "inconveniences."

The specific mechanism for increasing success is self-talk. *Self-talk* refers to the messages we communicate to ourselves. When an event occurs, such as our boss criticizing us on a task, we can use positive self-talk or negative self-talk. This results in either a positive or a negative feeling or behavior. To quote one source: "The difference between a really good day and a really awful day is not in what happened but in what you tell yourself about that day" (Whiteman et al., 1996, p. 196). (See also Turkington, 1998.)

Language does two important things. First, it serves as an aid to memory. It makes memory more efficient by allowing us to code events as verbal categories. Researchers have shown, for example, that we find it easier to recognize colors of low codability again if we named them for ourselves the first time we saw them (Brown and Lenneberg, 1954). It is now believed that an adult's memory is primarily verbal. And second, language also enables us to abstract indefinitely from our experience, which is especially important in communicating about abstract relationships (something animals are unable to do).

Language Problems

Ideally, language is a valuable instrument of thought; yet we know that language can sometimes interfere with our ability to think critically. Although Whorf was best known for his writings on linguistics, he was trained as an engineer. When he became an accident investigator, he began to realize that a certain percentage of accidents occurred as a result of what might be called "careless thinking." For example, people would be very careful around barrels labeled "gasoline" but would smoke unconcernedly around barrels labeled "empty gasoline barrel," though the fumes in the empty barrels were more likely to ignite than the actual gasoline (Whorf, 1956, p. 135). There are many ways in which an imprecise use of language interferes with our thought processes. We shall examine several that have a direct influence on our communication.

Abstract Language

When people use **abstract** language, they frequently cause communication difficulties that have to do with the *vagueness* of words. As concepts become more vague, or abstract, it gets harder and harder to decode the intended meaning. S. I. Hayakawa has written several books on semantics, and in one he included the so-called abstraction ladder we see in Figure 3.2.

In general, the more abstract the term, the greater our chances of misunderstanding. Consider this exchange between father and teenage son:

Father: Have a good time, and don't stay out late.

Son: Thanks, I will. Don't worry. I'll be home early.

The next day they may get into a disagreement because they were not thinking the same things when they used the words "early" and "late." Perhaps the son purposely did not clarify what the father meant by "late" because he didn't want to be held to a strict time limit. And the father may have been vague intentionally so that his son would have a chance to exercise judgment and learn to become more adult. On the other hand, if the son came home at 4:00 A.M., both father and son would probably agree that he had indeed stayed out "late."

Speaking of being more adult, how old is an adult? Do you become an adult when you are allowed to drive? Is it when you are allowed to drink? Is it when

Figure 3.2 *Abstraction Ladder*

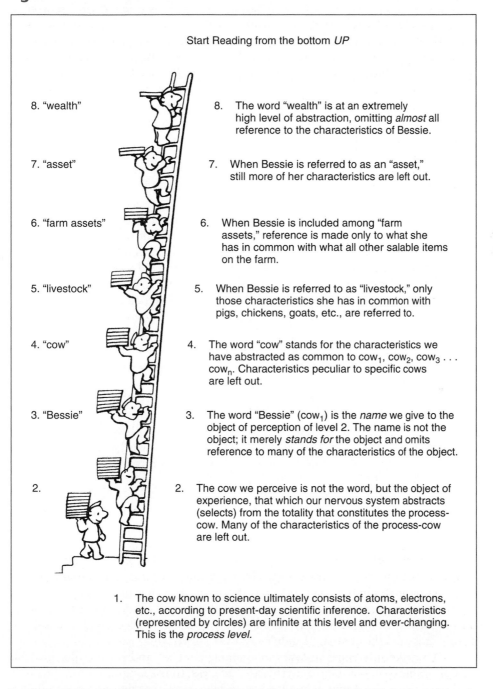

Start Reading from the bottom *UP*

8. "wealth"

8. The word "wealth" is at an extremely high level of abstraction, omitting *almost* all reference to the characteristics of Bessie.

7. "asset"

7. When Bessie is referred to as an "asset," still more of her characteristics are left out.

6. "farm assets"

6. When Bessie is included among "farm assets," reference is made only to what she has in common with what all other salable items on the farm.

5. "livestock"

5. When Bessie is referred to as "livestock," only those characteristics she has in common with pigs, chickens, goats, etc., are referred to.

4. "cow"

4. The word "cow" stands for the characteristics we have abstracted as common to cow_1, cow_2, cow_3 . . . cow_n. Characteristics peculiar to specific cows are left out.

3. "Bessie"

3. The word "Bessie" (cow_1) is the *name* we give to the object of perception of level 2. The name is not the object; it merely *stands for* the object and omits reference to many of the characteristics of the object.

2.

2. The cow we perceive is not the word, but the object of experience, that which our nervous system abstracts (selects) from the totality that constitutes the process-cow. Many of the characteristics of the process-cow are left out.

1. The cow known to science ultimately consists of atoms, electrons, etc., according to present-day scientific inference. Characteristics (represented by circles) are infinite at this level and ever-changing. This is the *process level*.

Source: From *Language in Thought and Action*, 4th ed. by S. I. Hayakawa, © 1978. Reprinted with permission of Heinle & Heinle, a division of Thomson Learning. Fax 800-730-2215.

you are allowed to see "adult" movies? Or is it when you become financially independent? In our society, the term "adult" is variously defined, and the age at which such privileges are granted varies.

Often, in an attempt to avoid ambiguity, we use very precise wording to clarify meaning. Legal contracts are such an example. But no amount of care is sufficient to avoid all ambiguity of interpretation. We need only look at the differences in how Supreme Court justices have interpreted the Constitution, or at the different ways in which the Bible has been interpreted, to see the inherent ambiguity in our use of language. Keep in mind the abstraction ladder, however, for some terms are considerably more abstract, and therefore more subject to misinterpretation, than others.

Inferences

An **inference** is *a conclusion or judgment derived from evidence or assumptions*. Every day you make dozens of inferences. When you sit down, you infer that the chair will support your weight. When you go through a green light, you infer that the traffic moving at right angles to you will stop at the red light. When you drive down a one-way street, you infer that all the traffic will be going in one direction. You may have good reason to expect these inferences to be correct, but there is also some uncalculated probability that events will not go as you expect. Drivers who have been involved in traffic accidents frequently say that the accident occurred because they inferred that the other party would act in a certain way when in fact he or she did not. Every year we read of people who were accidentally shot with guns they inferred were not loaded.

As students of communication, we are concerned with the inferences implicit in verbal messages. If you say, "It is sunny outside today," your statement can be easily verified. It is a factual statement based on an observed and verifiable event. If you say, "It is sunny outside; therefore, it is sunny fifty miles from here," you draw a conclusion based on more than what you have observed. You have made a statement based in part on an inference.

Consider a more complex situation. Sheila Waring has broken off a substantial part of one of her front teeth. Her dentist takes an x-ray, covers the tooth with a temporary, and gives her an appointment for the following week; she may, he mentions, need root canal work. The next week Sheila returns, and as she walks into the office, the dentist says, "I'm sorry, Sheila, You do need root canal work. This calls for a heroic effort." Hearing this, Sheila is terrified and during the next hour sits in the chair awaiting the awful pain that never comes. "There. Finished—" says the dentist, "I've taken out the nerve." "But I didn't feel it at all. I thought you said I would have to be heroic about it." "No. I said 'a heroic effort,'" answers the dentist. "I didn't say *your* effort."

We make inferences in every imaginable context, and it is neither possible nor desirable to avoid them entirely. Nevertheless, to use language more precisely and to be more discerning when we hear others speak, we should learn to distinguish between factual and inferential statements. "You spend a great deal of time with my roommate" is a statement of fact. It involves a low level of uncertainty, it is made as a result of direct observation, and it can be verified. Add to it "I'm sure he won't mind if you borrow his coat," and you have an inferential statement that may well jeopardize a friendship. In becoming more conscious of inference making, we can at least learn to calculate the risks involved.

To compound the problem, our language is structured so that no distinction is made between facts and inferences. It is the verb "to be" that creates the difficulty: there is no grammatical distinction made between a fact verified through sense data (e.g., "She is wearing a red coat") and a statement that cannot be verified through sense data and is merely an inference (e.g., "She is thinking about her upcoming date this weekend").

Dichotomies

Dichotomies, or *polar words,* are frequently responsible for another type of language problem. Some semanticists classify English as a "two-valued" rather than a "multivalued language." By this they mean that English has an excess of polar words and a relative scarcity of words to describe the wide middle ground between these opposites. Obviously, every person, entity, or event can be described in terms of a whole array of adjectives ranging from very favorable to very unfavorable. (Recall the Semantic Differential, discussed earlier in this chapter, which uses a seven-interval scale.) Yet we tend to say that a student is a "success" or a "failure," that a child is "good" or "bad," that a woman is "attractive" or "unattractive." Try, for example, to think of some words to describe the spots marked on the continua in the scale of dichotomies in Figure 3.3. As you search for words, you begin to see that there are a lot of distinctions for which we lack single words. The continua also illustrate how our language suggests that certain categories of experience are mutually exclusive, when in truth they are not.

Consider the first set of terms, "success" and "failure." Every human being undoubtedly meets with some success and some failure during the course of a lifetime. An insurance broker unemployed for many months and unable to find work may also be a supportive and much-loved father and husband. Yet our language suggests that he be classified as either a success or a failure. Similar difficulties crop up if we are asked to apply such adjectives as "brilliant" and "stupid" or "winner" and "loser" to other people. Is the math major with a straight A average brilliant or stupid if she can't learn to drive a car or ride a bike? If the author of a recent best-seller is divorced for the third time, is he a winner or a loser?

When polar terms are used in a misleading way, they suggest false dichotomies, reducing experience in a way that it need not be reduced. Differences are emphasized and similarities are overlooked, and in the process a great deal of information is lost. This is certainly true in our country at election time.

One way to avoid making false dichotomies, as Haney (1973, p. 374) has pointed out, is to make use of the questions "How much?" and "To what extent?":

Figure 3.3

SCALE OF DICHOTOMIES

Success	—	—	X	—	—	— Failure
Brilliant	—	—	—	X	—	— Stupid
Handsome	—	—	X	—	—	— Ugly
Winner	—	—	—	X	—	— Loser
Honest	—	—	—	X	—	— Dishonest
Black	—	X	—	—	—	— White

Source: Reprinted from the *Journal of Applied Behavioral Science*, 6, "The Fifth Achievement," p. 418, copyright © 1970, with permission from Elsevier Science.

How much of a success am I?

How much of a change is this from his former stand on gun control?

To *what extent* is he honest?

To *what extent* is her plan practical?

With the aid of such questions, perhaps we can keep in mind that we have many options, that we need not cast our messages in black-and-white terms, and that we need not accept these either-or distinctions when they are made by others.

Euphemisms

Through **euphemisms** we *substitute mild, vague, or less emotionally charged terms for more blunt ones*—"campaign of disinformation" for "smear campaign," "security review procedure" for "censorship," "discomfort" for "pain," "memory garden" for "cemetery," "powder room" for "bathroom," "attack" for "rape." "Portly," "stout," and "heavy-set" are ways to avoid saying "fat." Of course, they lack the specificity of "fat" as well as the affect attached to the word. If we hear that a woman was "attacked," we don't know if she was assaulted or raped. Often the problem created by using euphemisms is that the intent may be conveyed but not the degree to which the intent is felt. So-called empty words are euphemisms because they are pleasant sounding yet indirect enough to avoid being blunt: "nice," "wonderful," and "pleasant" appear to be all-purpose euphemisms. They make for dull conversations. And on many occasions, euphemistic language is used to misrepresent what is being said. For example, one high school counselor revealed several phrases he used in writing student recommendations for college applications: describing a student with serious emotional problems as "having peaks and valleys"; saying a student "likes to take risks" when referring to a drug problem; characterizing an arrogant student as "pushing against the limits" (Carmody, 1989, p. B6).

In a study of encoding, Motley gives these examples of intentional ambiguity and euphemism:

[Thinking] *The (roommate's) manuscript is nonsensical.*

[Saying] *It's different.*

[Thinking] *The child is a brat.*

[Saying] *That's quite a kid.*

(Adapted from Motley, 1992, p. 309)

Equivocal Language

Misunderstandings often occur because people assume that a word, a phrase, or even a sentence is unequivocal—that is, it has only one meaning. Hayakawa refers to this as "the 'one word, one meaning' fallacy" (1978). But much of the language we use is **equivocal**; it has *two or more possible interpretations.*

We've seen the problems created by disagreements over the referents of such words as "peace," "truth," and "freedom." Misunderstandings are also quite common when the words and phrases in question sound far more concrete. If your date says, "Let's get a drink after the show," the drink may refer to an alcoholic beverage, continuing the evening in a club, or simply a desire to stay together for simple conversation.

Newspaper columnist William Safire recalls receiving an invitation to the opera. "The time, date, and place were briskly and neatly laid out, and then, in the corner, a mysterious instruction about dress: '*Not Black Tie.*' What is that supposed to mean?":

Profound motives aside, does *not black tie* mean business suit, which is what it says on the Turkish Embassy's invitation to a reception? Taking it a step further . . . does that mean today's American Uniform (blue blazer, beige pants) is out? Does *not black tie* mean "any old tie" or "no tie at all"? (1990, p. 84)

There seem to be two sources of confusion about words or phrases. First, people may assume that because they are using the same word, they agree, when in fact each interprets the word differently. In a comical incident, a woman asks a pharmacist for a refill of her prescription for "the pill." "Please hurry," she adds, "I've got someone waiting in the car." Much humor is based on such double meanings. In daily communication this type of confusion may not be so funny.

For example, one of the authors and spouse—and we're not saying which one—were drawn into a needless argument:

Husband:	You know, the travel literature on Switzerland that I borrowed is still in the house. Since we're not going, I'd better return it to that fellow in my office. Could you get it together for me so I can take it in tomorrow?
Wife:	I don't know where it is.
Husband:	What kind of answer is that? If it's too much trouble, forget it.
Wife:	What do you mean, "What kind of answer is that?" How can I do anything with it if I can't find it?
Husband:	There's nothing to do. All I asked you to do was find it. You don't have to give me a smart answer.
Wife:	But you said "get it together." I thought you meant put it in some sort of order.
Husband:	I meant "find it." Don't you know what "get it together" means?
Wife:	Well, I didn't know it meant that.
Husband:	If you didn't know, why didn't you ask me?
Wife:	Because I thought I knew. I speak English, too, you know.

For a time this misunderstanding created a lot of ill feeling. Both husband and wife were insulted—the husband because he felt his wife had refused to do something relatively simple for him, and the wife because she felt her husband had insulted her intelligence.

A second type of misunderstanding occurs when two people assume that they disagree because they are using different words when actually they may agree on the concept or entity represented by those words. That is, they use different terms that have the same referent. For example, a school psychologist and a guidance counselor were discussing a student who was failing several of her classes though she was of above-average intelligence. A disagreement developed when the counselor insisted that the girl definitely needed "help." "She certainly does not," countered the psychologist. "She needs psychological intervention." "That's what I'm saying," said the counselor. "She should be getting psychological counseling." "Well, then we agree," answered the psychologist. "When you said 'help,' I thought you were talking about tutoring." The psychologist and counselor were able to resolve their apparent differences because they did stop and redefine their terms.

Although our attention has been given to words or phrases, most messages take the form of sentences. "It's a rainy day," remarks Jack to Jill. What could be clearer than the meaning of that sentence? Yet Laing (1972) suggests five ways in which Jack might intend his statement. Perhaps he wishes to register the fact that it is a rainy day. If yesterday Jack and Jill agreed to go for a walk instead of going to a movie, he might be saying that because of the rain he will probably get to see the movie. He might be implying that because of the weather Jill should stay at home. If yesterday the two argued about what the weather would be like, he might mean that Jill is right again or that he is the one who always predicts the weather correctly. If the window is open, he might be saying that he would like Jill to close it. No doubt each of us could come up with several other interpretations. The point is that any message derives a great part of its meaning from the context in which it is transmitted. Our knowledge of the speaker and the speaker's use of language, our own associations with the words he or she chooses, our previous relationship, and the messages we have already exchanged should all play a part in how we interpret what is said.

Culture as Our Frame of Reference

Although all our behaviors have possible meaning for a receiver, language is by far our most explicit form of communication. In using it, our desire is to facilitate thought, not to obscure it. Language is potentially the most precise vehicle we have for human communication. Even if we grant the infinite richness of language and the precision it is capable of expressing, however, a look at intercultural communication makes clear that often people are divided not because of a failure to understand grammar or vocabulary but because of a failure to understand rhetoric or point of view.

Kenneth Kaunda, the former president of Zambia, insists that Westerners and Africans have very different ways of seeing things, solving problems, and thinking in general. He characterizes the Westerner as having a "problem-solving mind." Once a Westerner perceives a problem, he or she feels compelled to solve it. Unable to live with contradictory ideas, the Westerner excludes all solutions that have no logical basis. Supernatural and nonrational phenomena are regarded as superstition. The African, on the other hand, allows himself or herself to experience all phenomena, nonrational as well as rational. The African has a "situation-experiencing mind." Kaunda believes that "the African can hold contradictory ideas in fruitful tension within his mind without any sense of incongruity, and he will act on the basis of the one which seems most appropriate to the particular situation" (Legum, 1976, pp. 63–64).

In ancient India, according to Kirkwood (1989) and other students of Indian rhetoric, truthfulness was considered the prime standard for speech. Emphasis was placed not only on the value of truthful speech to listeners but on the profound effects for the speaker as well. The practice of speaking truthfully was regarded as spiritually liberating, and the performance itself—the act of speaking the truth—brought with it self-knowledge as well as freedom, thus transforming the speaker. Such ideas date back to the tenth century B.C. and are an enduring aspect of India's culture.

On the other hand, a study of Chinese and Japanese attitudes toward speech communication in public settings offers several reasons for the lack of argumentation and debate in the Far East (Becker, 1991). According to Becker, social history contributed to an aversion to public debate. For example, in the Chinese and Japanese traditions, "taking opposite sides of an argument necessarily meant becoming a personal rival and antagonist of the one who held the other side. The more important concomitant of this idea was that if one did not wish to become a lifelong opponent of someone else, he would not venture an opinion contrary to the other person's opinions in public. Even the legal system was set up in such a way that it avoided direct confrontations" (p. 236).

In addition, various linguistic features of Chinese and Japanese (e.g., Chinese lacks plurals and tenses) as well as great differences between Western and Eastern philosophy and religion all presented powerful barriers to the widespread use of debate and argumentation for considering new proposals or strategies for implementing social and political change (Becker, 1991, p. 242). Becker emphasizes that the Westerner's ideal speech situation requiring "equality of participants, freedom from social coercion, suspension of privilege, and free expression of feeling . . . [would be] both impractical and even theoretically inconceivable to traditionally educated Chinese and Japanese" (p. 242).

In looking at different cultural frames of reference, we seem to have come full circle, recalling elements of the Sapir-Whorf hypothesis. To some degree, linguistic traditions help shape our thought processes, but for members of different cultures, traditions can be a barrier.

We've considered several language-related problems that interfere with your ability to think and communicate clearly. Of course, there are numerous others. But just being aware of the *possibility* that language can be a source of misunderstanding should enable you to be more perceptive about verbal messages.

WORDS IN ACTION

In this final section of our chapter, we will examine some ways in which words influence human actions, both directly and indirectly. In ancient times, people of many diverse cultures believed that words had magical powers. For example, in ancient Egypt a man received two names: his true name, which he concealed, and his good name, by which he was known publicly. Even today many primitive societies regard words as magical. Members of some cultures go to great lengths to conceal their personal names. They avoid saying the names of their gods. The names of their dead are never uttered. Presumably, we moderns are far more sophisticated. Yet we have our own verbal taboos. And the euphemisms we've just talked about are part of our everyday vocabulary. Thus, we often hear not that someone "died" but that he or she "passed away." And a sudden drop in the stock market is often termed a "correction."

Recently, the use of the term "mother" has come into some controversy. According to one source, "In Massachusetts and many other states, only the woman who gives birth is presumed to be the mother and can have her name on the original birth certificate. The law does not address women becoming mothers by having embryos implanted in a surrogate . . . More than a month after they were born, a baby boy and his twin sister still have no birth certificates. The paperwork is being held up in a dispute over the legal definition of the term mother" (Lavoie, 2001, p. A7).

Some empirical studies of word power examine the ways in which a speaker's use of profane words affects our judgment of his or her credibility. (See Chapter 13 for a discussion of credibility.) Three classes of profanity were used: religious, excretory, and sexual. Although religious profanity was less offensive when circumstances appeared to justify it, sexual profanity—whether provoked or unprovoked—always seemed to bring the speakers significantly lower credibility ratings. These results are surprisingly consistent: They are the same for males and females, older and younger women, and freshmen and graduate students (Rossiter and Bostrom, 1968; Bostrom et al., 1973; Mabry, 1975).

Writers on public communication traditionally refer to the effective use of language as "eloquence." In public speaking, eloquence describes a more dramatic, stirring use of language—often for the purpose of inspiring or persuading others. For example, recently Rev. James Forbes of Manhattan, a "preacher's preacher" who is known for his eloquence, spoke before a group of ministers on the need for compassion in preaching about AIDS. "In an existential sense," he said, "we all have AIDS, and the question is how we want to be treated as dying men and women" (Goldman, 1989, p. B3). One thinks also of the famous speech of Dr. Martin Luther King, Jr., "I Have a Dream," through which thousands were inspired to work for equal rights:

> I have a dream that one day, even the state of Mississippi, a state sweltering with the heat of injustice, sweltering with the heat of oppression, will be transformed into an oasis of freedom and justice. . . .
>
> With this faith we will be able to hew out of the mountain of despair a stone of hope. With this faith we will be able to transform the jangling discords of our nation into a beautiful symphony of brotherhood.

With these words, Dr. King was able to move people's feelings more powerfully than he could have with more commonplace language. Lamenting the "eloquence gap" in contemporary politics, poet Michael Blumenthal expressed his sense that "a nation that no longer expects and demands eloquence and statesmanship from its politicians no longer expects and demands grandeur from itself—or precision of belief from those who lead it" (1989, p. 18).

Sometimes our decisions are based in part on how a thing is labeled. For example, certain words clearly have greater prestige than others. A "classic car" is better than an old one. "Vintage clothing" is more appealing than old secondhand clothing. The same desk commands different prices when it is called "used," "secondhand," or "antique." "Doctor" is another powerful word. In many situations, for example, it is undeniable that "Dr." Bradley will get more attention than "Ms." Bradley or "Mr." Bradley.

Sexist Language

Since the late 1960s many students of language, a good many feminists among them, have argued that our language is sexist, that it reflects a bias affecting how women are perceived and treated by others and sometimes how they regard themselves. For example, words associated with the descriptions of males often have positive connotations—"confident," "forceful," "strong," and the like—whereas females are more often described as "fickle," "frivolous," "timid," and so forth (Heilbrun, 1976).

In studies at three different universities, Pearson and her associates (1991) found that when students were asked to list all the terms for men and women, the list of words for women was longer and generally much less favorable than the one for men. (See Table 3.1.) It's the group in power, these writers point out, that "typically does the naming or labeling. In our culture men tend to name people, places, and things."

Of the differences in the labeling of men and women, Pearson et al. note, "names for women are sometimes created by adding another word or a feminine marker to a name for men" (thus, "waitress," "actress," and so on). In addition, terms for women tend to be more frequently sexual, often with connotations that the women are the objects of sexual conquest.

New York Times columnist Anna Quindlen (1992) comments on another label:

> At the time of Anita Hill's testimony, a waitress told me of complaining to the manager of the coffee shop in which she worked about his smutty comments and intimate pats. He replied, "You're a skirt." Then he told her that if she didn't like it, there were plenty of other skirts out there who would take the job—and the abuse. (p. 19)

The metaphors used for men and women also differ. Metaphors involving food are often used when referring to women—"tomato," "cookie," "sugar," "piece of cake," and so on. Sometimes animal names are used in referring to women, but these tend to be the names of baby animals ("chick" or "kitty," for example)—names that connote weakness or vulnerability. If men are linked with animals, it's with the names of far more powerful animals ("wolf" is an example). Pearson et al. (1991) point out that the terms for men and women are often polar opposites with the male term being positive, the female term negative; "bachelor" and "old maid" are a case in point.

Women tend to be referred to by euphemisms far more frequently than men are. And although men are not often called "gentlemen" or "boys," "ladies" and "girls" are terms still frequently heard by women as forms of address. Women use them too—hence such comments as "I'm going out for lunch with the girls."

A more subtle but extremely influential form of sexist language is the high frequency of familiar—or overly familiar—terms applied to women, terms that reflect lower social status. Although men are more frequently addressed formally

Table 3.1	Terms for Women and Men			
Women			**Men**	
Chick	Wife	Honey	Gent	Boy
Girl	Old maid	Madam	Man	Stud
Old lady	Bitch	Whore	Guy	Hunk
Piece	Lady	Dog	Male	Bastard
Female	Broad	Cow	Husband	
Prostitute	Woman	Old biddy		

Source: From *Gender and Communication,* by Judy Cornelia Pearson, 1985. Reprinted by permission of the author.

("Sir," "Mister," and so on), it is quite common for women to be called by their first names, or even to hear themselves called "honey," "hon," "baby," "sweetie," "dear," or the like—and sometimes by people they've never met before (Pearson et al., 1991, p. 100).

Despite many reforms, by far the most blatant example of sexist language is still the use of "man" as the generic term for "people" or "humanity," and along with this goes the frequent use of the personal pronoun "his"—especially in expository writing—as though women were pretty much an afterthought. In the last decade, the use of such variants as "his or her," "he/she," "his/her," and "he or she" became more widespread. One critic writing on gender formulates the problem this way:

> The abstract form, the general, the universal, this is what the so-called masculine gender means, for the class of men have appropriated the universal for themselves. One must understand that men are not born with a faculty for the universal and that women are not reduced at birth to the particular. The universe has been, and is, continually, at every moment, appropriated by men. (Wittig, 1986, p. 66)

The implication that men are the more important members of the human race can be changed in many ways. For example, "manhood" may be replaced by the term "adulthood," "firemen" by "firefighters," and so on. The use of such words as "chairperson," "business person," and "he/she"—for all their attendant awkwardness—attempts to address this problem.

The insistence of many groups on such changes is legitimate because, as we have tried to indicate, words shape perceptions and self-concepts. Linguistic changes evolve slowly, but they are taking place.

Male and Female Language Usage

Are there true differences between the way males and females use language? Most research supports the stereotypic view that in contrast to males, females are more submissive, affected by social pressure, and responsive to the needs of others. It has been found that, although women seem to respond more to the remarks of other people, work harder at maintaining conversations, and give more "positive minimal responses," it is men who generally initiate as well as receive more interaction. Men also interrupt others more and ignore the remarks of others more frequently than women do. Such differences are often explained in terms of the greater social power men enjoy in most communication contexts (B. J. Haslett, 1987, p. 216).

Language differences that give rise to these perceptions have been described in this way: Females use more words, more intensifiers, questions, including tag questions ("That's great, isn't it?"), and affect words (i.e., words implying emotion) than males use (Berryman and Wilcox, 1980). Male speech, on the other hand, shows more instances of incorrect grammar, obscenities, and slang (Liska et al., 1981). Apparently both males and females expect males to use more verbally aggressive strategies and females to use strategies that are more social and less verbally aggressive (Burgoon et al., 1983).

There are contrary findings worth noting, however. According to a study of college students, males and females differ little in the amount or quality of their talk about emotions, but males use more affect words when talking to females than to males; female speech does not vary this way (Shimanoff, 1988). A second study found that males and females used the same number of qualifiers ("maybe," "sort of," and the like) when talking to males, but males, when talking to females, decreased the number of qualifiers (Martin and Craig, 1983). Although language differences between men and women exist, such usage seems to be context-bound. As research in this area continues, it is likely that more and more conclusions will be qualified.

In *You Just Don't Understand,* a popular book that became a national bestseller, sociolinguist Deborah Tannen (1990) proposes that communication difficulties between men and women often originate in gender differences in conversational style.

She makes the distinction between "report talk" and "rapport talk." Tannen argues that most men use conversation primarily as a language of **report,** that is, "as *a means to preserve independence and negotiate and maintain status in a hierarchical social order*" (1990, p. 77). This conversational style emphasizes demonstrating knowledge and skill and in general having the right information. "From childhood," writes Tannen, "men learn to use talking as a way to get and keep attention" (p. 77). Thus in the world of many men, "conversations are negotiations in which people try to achieve the upper hand if they can, and protect themselves from others' attempts to push them down and push them around" (p. 24).

To most women conversation is, for the most part, "a language of **rapport,**" with which they have learned since childhood to *establish connections and negotiate relationships, often for greater closeness.* What women emphasize in their talk are their similarities with other people and their comparable experiences ("I'm just like that," "The same thing happened to me . . ."). Women also have interests in achievement or status goals, says Tannen (1990), but they tend to go after them "in the guise of connection." Similarly,

> Men are also concerned with achieving involvement and avoiding isolation, but they are not focused on these goals, and they tend to pursue them in the guise of opposition. (p. 25)

According to Tannen, it's these differences in style that account for so many mis- understandings. She gives a striking example:

> Though both women and men complain of being interrupted by each other, the behaviors they are complaining about are different.
> In many of the comments I heard from people I interviewed, men felt interrupted by women who overlapped with words of agreement and support and anticipation of how their sentences and thoughts would end. If a woman supported a man's story by elaborating on a point different from the one he had intended, he felt his right to tell his own story had been violated. (p. 210)

Feminist critic Deborah Cameron identifies two current approaches to the language styles of men and women. She contrasts theories of **difference,** such as Tannen's, with theories of **dominance.** In theories of dominance, "Women's style is seen as the outcome of power struggles and negotiations . . . played out under the surface of conversation" (1990, p. 25). This, for example, is how a theory of dominance would interpret research findings about questions:

> Women ask more questions than men . . . not because insecurity is part of [their] psychology and therefore of [their] speech style . . . but because men in a dominant position often refuse to take responsibility for the smooth conduct of interpersonal relations . . . Asking them a question is thus an effective strategy for forcing them to acknowledge and contribute to the talk. It can be argued that features like question-asking are not deferential at all . . . (p. 25)

Theories such as these are a source of spirited debate and will be most valu- able if they generate further research in language studies.

Powerful and Powerless Language

As we speak, many of us use tag questions—for example, "Let's go to the movies, okay?"—in making simple statements. We also use hedges—"kinda" and "I think"—or disclaimers such as "I probably shouldn't say this" and "I'm not really sure." In examining seven message types of differing **power,** Bradac and Mulac (1984) found that the language forms just described as well as hesitations such as "uh" and "well" are perceived by other people as forms of powerless and ineffective speech; on the other hand, speech free of such usage is considered both powerful and effective.

A more recent study explored the relationship between language style and gender stereotypes (Quina et al., 1987). Researchers found that individuals using a so-called feminine style of speech characterized by politeness, exaggeration, hedging, and illogical sequence—one that was generally nonassertive—were perceived as having greater warmth but less competence than those having a "masculine" style. The authors remind us that "a polite, warm linguistic style is not consistent with the popular image of American corporate success or achievement" (p. 118). Nonetheless, qualities associated with a feminine style included sensitivity, friendliness, and sincerity.

In general, communicators who use a powerful style are considered more competent and attractive. Legal situations are different, however; plaintiffs and defendants using a more powerful style are also considered more blameworthy, perhaps because they seem "in control" of themselves. Less powerful speakers are more often seen as victims (Bradac et al., 1981).

But it is not always the language itself that reveals who is powerful: The information provided by context as well as the personalities of those involved must also be considered. For example, the boss who asks the secretary to type something, by using several powerless forms such as hesitations, hedges, and tag questions, may appear polite and social—not powerless—even though he or she makes the request sound less like a demand (Bradac, 1983).

Metacommunication

In addition to trying to use a more powerful language, there's another very important way to increase the effectiveness of verbal messages. With practice, you can use language to change your relationship to others through **metacommunication**—that is, *communication about communication.* This is a concept closely linked to the relationship level of human encounters. For example, if you say to your mother, "Tell him to mind his own damned business," and she replies, "I wish you wouldn't swear so much. You do it more and more, and I don't like it," she is responding not to the content of your remark but to your method of getting your point across. The content of her communication is communication itself.

Any comment directed at the way in which a person communicates is an example of metacommunication. For years the procedure in public-speaking classes has been for students to give practice speeches and then have the instructor and class members give their reactions to the speaker and the speech. Such comments as "I thought you had excellent examples," "You could have brought out your central idea more explicitly," and "Try to be a little more enthusiastic" are all instances of metacommunicating.

Writing about families, Galvin and Brommel (1991) observe:

Metacommunication occurs when people communicate about their communication, when they give verbal and nonverbal instructions about how their messages should be understood. Such remarks as "I was only kidding," "This is important," or "Talking about this makes me uncomfortable" are signals to another on how to interpret certain comments, as are facial expressions, gestures, or vocal tones." (p. 18)

Metacommunication is not always explicit, even when it is verbal. Sometimes conversations that begin at the content level become forms of metacommunication. We can best illustrate with an anecdote. Craig and Jeanne, dressed for a night on the town, have just stepped out of a cab. As they stand at the corner waiting for the light to change, they rapidly become involved in a heated argument:

Jeanne: Next time try to pick me up earlier so we can be on time.

Craig: It's only a party. Next time tell me beforehand if you think it's so important to be there at eight sharp. And don't sound so annoyed.

Jeanne: But you're always late.

Craig: I'm not always late. Don't generalize like that.

Jeanne: Well, you're late a lot of the time. Why do you always put me down when I say something about you?

Craig: I don't "always" put you down. There you go again, generalizing.

Although they may well remember it simply as a quarrel about lateness, Craig and Jeanne are arguing about how they communicate with each other. He tells her not to sound so annoyed, he informs her that she makes too many generalizations, she counters that he puts her down, and so on. In effect, they are arguing about their relationship.

As we will see in Chapter 6, when there are serious conflicts about relationships rather than content, metacommunication is often especially difficult (Sillars and Weisberg, 1987). Two people may lack the skill to use metacommunication; and the source of the conflict may be "diffuse and selectively perceived. Attempts to communicate are therefore frustrated by a failure to agree on the definition of the conflict and by an ability to metacommunicate" (p. 151).

In a more supportive situation, the use of metacommunication might help people become aware of ways in which their communication practices are ineffective. For example, one teenage girl finally confided to her mother that she was embarrassed when the mother tried to sound "hip" in front of the daughter's teenage friends. It is sometimes awkward to provide such feedback. When given in a kind rather than a hostile way, however, it can be a valuable impetus to self-improvement.

Summary

Our analysis of verbal communication began with a consideration of the concept of meaning. In discussing the symbolic nature of language, we saw that symbols and referents are associated with each other only by convention and that it is human beings who assign meanings to words. We reviewed the traditional distinction between denotation and connotation and went on to suggest that it might be more useful to distinguish between private and shared meanings. In this connection, we discussed overlapping linguistic codes and codeswitching.

Our second subject was message encoding, which we approached through a comparison of the encoding abilities of children and adults. Piaget's research on socialized and egocentric speech made it clear that the message sender's perceptions and expectations about the receiver affect his or her ability to communicate accurately. While Piaget viewed the child's speech as predominantly egocentric, most theorists and researchers have come to view the child as sociocentric from birth with competence in communication developing through interaction that begins in infancy. In this alternate view, the adult caretaker (the mother, in most Western cultures) plays a critical role in developing the child's conversational abilities.

Our next concern was the relationship between thought and language, and after examining the Sapir-Whorf hypothesis, we considered several language problems created through abstracting, inferences, dichotomies, euphemisms, and equivocal meanings. We went on to observe that when people of different cultures communicate, they may be separated not so much by grammar or vocabulary as by frame of reference.

To study words in action, we examined sexist language, differences between males and females in their use of language (these seem to be context-bound), and the language forms perceived by others as powerful or powerless. In closing, we saw that metacommunication (communication *about* communication) is potentially a means of improving one's relationships.

Go to the Online Learning Center at www.mhhe.com/ tubbsmoss for glossary flashcards and crossword puzzles.

Key Terms

Connotation
Cultural frame of reference
Denotation

Encoding
Metacommunication
Sapir-Whorf hypothesis

Sexist language
Shared Meanings

For further review, go to the Self-Quiz on the Online Learning Center at www.mhhe.com/ tubbsmoss.

Review Questions

1.   What is intended by the statement "The word is not the thing"?

2.   What is the difference between denotation and connotation?

3.   What is the Semantic Differential? Give an example of a differential.

4.   Explain the difference between private and shared meanings.

5.   What are the concepts of overlapping codes and codeswitching?

6.   Explain Piaget's theory about how the child uses language.

7.   Discuss the current view that the child is sociocentric from birth and that communication develops out of interaction.

8.   What is the Sapir-Whorf hypothesis?

9.   Discuss two ways in which language affects thought.

10.   Describe the concept of abstracting and give examples.

11.   Describe at least four problem areas in our use of language. Give an example of each.

12.   What is the influence of viewpoint or frame of reference (as distinguished from grammar and vocabulary) on communication between cultures? Give two examples.

13.   Discuss the use of sexist language and give two examples.

14.   What are some of the differences between how males and females use language?

15.   Specify the difference between the way males and females use language on the job.

16.   Identify powerful and powerless language and explain its relationship to communication style.

17.   What is metacommunication? Give an example.

Exercises

1.   a.   Construct a Semantic Differential consisting of ten bipolar adjectives. Assess the potential marketability of a fictitious product name by asking several classmates to react to two or more names using the Semantic Differential. The sample scale below shows two names for a perfume.

Bouquet		Summer Nights	
Good X __ __ __ __ __ __ Bad		Good __ __ __ __ __ X __ Bad	
Sharp __ X __ __ __ __ __ Dull		Sharp __ __ __ __ __ __ X Dull	
Active __ __ __ X __ __ __ Passive		Active __ __ __ X __ __ __ Passive	
Pretty __ __ X __ __ __ __ Ugly		Pretty __ __ __ X __ __ __ Ugly	

      b.   How do the responses on the Semantic Differential reflect the difference between denotation and connotation; between private and shared meaning?

2.   Construct a two-column list with proper names in one column and stereotypical occupations associated with those names in the second. Mix up the order of names and occupations in each column. Present the lists to several people and ask them to match the names and occupations. A sample list appears follows:

Miss Flora	Ballet dancer
Spencer Turnbull	Teacher
Harry Hogan	Car thief
Speedy	Banker
Dominique Dubois	Hairdresser
Ken Sharp	Wrestling coach

a. To what extent do people agree in their responses? How do the results relate to the statement "The word is not the thing"?

b. How do the results relate to the three factors that affect stereotype perceptions (see Chapter 2)?

c. What implications do these results suggest about the relationship between language, stereotyping, and communication effectiveness?

3. Interview two people who are ostensibly very different—a local politician and an artist, for example. Ask each of them to make a list of adjectives describing (a) himself or herself and (b) a member of the other group. Compare the lists to see how differently each group member perceives himself or herself from the way he or she is perceived by the other person. Notice how the perceptual differences are manifested in the words chosen for the descriptions.

4. Prepare an oral persuasive message in two forms. Use the most tactful language possible in one and the most inflammatory terms you can think of in the other. Give the messages to two groups, and try to assess their reactions on an attitude scale. Which message is more effective? If the audiences are similar and your messages alike except for word choice (and assuming the nonverbal cues are similar), any difference in your results should be due to the difference in the language you use.

5. In a chance conversation deliberately assume that individual words have only one meaning and try to interpret them in a way that the other person does not intend. What are the results?

6. Prepare a short presentation in two forms. In the first, use words that are high on the ladder of abstraction (i.e., vague); in the second, use much more concrete, highly specific words. Discuss class reactions to these different presentations.

Suggested Readings

Bate, Barbara, and Anita Taylor, eds. *Women Communicating*. Norwood, NJ: Ablex, 1988.

An important collection of studies on women's talk.

Bennett, William J. *The Death of Outrage*. New York: Free Press, 1998.

Analyzes the rhetoric of President William J. Clinton and analyzes his use and misuse of language.

Donnellon, Anne. *Team Talk: The Power of Language in Team Dynamics*. Cambridge: Harvard Business School Press, 1996.

This excellent book analyzes teams from the standpoint of their members' language. It offers an excellent framework for analyzing and improving teams.

www.slanguage.com

A website that monitors current and changing slang words and expressions. It specifically focuses on the slang terms used by Generation X.

Scotti, Anna, and Paul Young. *Buzzwords: L.A. Freespeak*. New York: St. Martin's Press, 1997.

Beautifully illustrates the ever-changing nature of language.

Tannen, Deborah. *The Argument Culture: Moving from Debate to Dialogue*. New York: Random House, 1998.

This outstanding author relates the use of language to improving communication in conflict situations. The book includes information on communication between genders, communication across cultures, and the role of technology.

The Nonverbal Message

4

Chapter Objectives

After reading this chapter, you should be able to:

1. Describe four categories of communication, distinguishing between verbal and nonverbal as well as vocal and nonvocal, and give an example of each.
2. Discuss the kinds of information conveyed by nonverbal and verbal messages and three ways in which they are related.
3. Discuss the concepts of personal space and interpersonal distance.
4. Explain how we communicate through our use of time and how timing can interfere with intercultural communication.
5. Identify the major visual cues given by facial expression and head and body movements, and discuss the kinds of messages they convey.
6. Describe how one's choice of physical objects, including clothing, communicates messages to others.
7. Explain the concept of paralinguistics and identify four kinds of vocal cues, giving an example of each.
8. Discuss deception cues and recent research findings on accuracy in judging deception and the mutual influence of deceivers and detectors.

In *Dinner with Friends*, a play about two married couples, Karen and Gabe are shocked to learn that their long-time friends, Beth and Tom, are getting a divorce. When Gabe tries to intervene and bring the two together again, he takes Tom aside and asks if their problem is about sex. Tom tells him it's not that. "So you're still making love, huh," says Gabe:

> *Tom:* I wouldn't exactly call it making love . . . Beth really wouldn't touch me much anymore.
>
> *Gabe:* What do you mean?
>
> *Tom:* I mean the way someone who loved you might casually slip a hand through your arm or onto your shoulder or something . . . I did an experiment. I decided I wasn't going to touch her and see how long it would take before she touched me. I'm not talking about sex now; I'm talking about skin-to-skin contact. A simple good night kiss, holding hands. She wouldn't touch me, Gabe. At all. I gave it a week. I couldn't stand it. I broke down and cried. (Margulies, 2000, p. 38–39)

Source: Excerpts from the play *Dinner with Friends* by Donald Margulies, Copyright © 2000 by the author. Published by Theatre Communications Group. Used by permission.

Through touch we sustain and intensify our sense of connection with others. How and when we use touch—or avoid it—is just one of the questions we will be examining in this chapter as we look at the broad spectrum of nonverbal communication behaviors.

We begin by considering the relative weight people give to verbal and nonverbal messages. Thus, we will look at how nonverbal messages are interpreted, what types of information we receive through them, and how they interact with verbal messages.

INTERPRETING NONVERBAL MESSAGES

The literal definition of nonverbal communication, communication without words, is something of an oversimplification, because written words are considered "verbal" although they lack the element of sound. Stewart and D'Angelo (1980) propose that if we distinguish verbal from nonverbal and vocal from nonvocal, we have four categories or types of communication. **Verbal/vocal communication** refers to *communication through the spoken word*. For example, Carolyn and her father discuss the new car Carolyn wants to buy and her plans for getting together the money. In **verbal/nonvocal communication**, *words are involved but no speaking takes place*: If she writes a letter to her father about the car, her communication is verbal but nonvocal. Or suppose that after she talks about the car, she asks her father for a loan and her father simply groans. Such *groans, or vocalizations, constitute a form of* **nonverbal/vocal communication**. A fourth kind of communication, **nonverbal/nonvocal communication**, *involves only gestures and appearance*—imagine Carolyn's father looking angry or pleased—or perhaps simply puzzled. Seen in these terms, **nonverbal communication** *conveys nonlinguistic messages*.